ROUGH
GUIDES

T0082176

POCKET **ROUGH GUIDE**
BARCELONA

this sixth edition updated by
SALLY DAVIES

CONTENTS

BARCELONA

It's tempting to say that there's nowhere quite like Barcelona – there's certainly no other city in Spain to touch it for sheer style, looks or energy. The glossy mags and travel press dwell enthusiastically on its outrageous architecture, designer shopping, cool bars and vibrant cultural scene, but Barcelona is more than just this year's fad. It's a confident, progressive city, one that is tirelessly self-renewing while preserving all that's best about its past. As old neighbourhoods bloom, and landmark museums and sights are restored with panache, there's still an enduring embrace of the good things in life, from the daily markets to the late-night cafés.

Casa Milà

Fundació Antoni Tàpies

The province of Catalunya (Catalonia in English), of which Barcelona is the capital, has a historical identity going back as far as the ninth century, and through the long period of domination by outside powers, as well as during the Franco dictatorship, it proved impossible to stifle the Catalan spirit. The city reflects this independence, being at the forefront of Spanish political activism, radical design and architecture, and commercial dynamism.

This is seen most perfectly in the glorious *modernista* (Art Nouveau) buildings that stud the city's streets and avenues. Antoni Gaudí is the most famous of those who have left their mark on Barcelona in this way: his Sagrada Família church is rightly revered, but just as fascinating are the (literally) fantastic houses, public buildings and parks that he and his contemporaries designed.

The city also boasts an extensive medieval Old Town – full of pivotal buildings from an earlier age of expansion – and a stupendous artistic legacy, from national (ie, Catalan) collections of Romanesque, Gothic and contemporary art to major galleries containing the life's work of the Catalan artists Joan Miró and Antoni Tàpies (not to mention a celebrated showcase of the work of Pablo Picasso).

Barcelona is equally proud of its cutting-edge restaurants – featuring

Best places for a Barcelona picnic

Parc de la Ciutadella is the city centre's favourite green space, while the gardens of Montjuïc offer some fantastic views. Any time the sun shines, the beach between Barceloneta and Port Olímpic makes for a great alfresco lunch, though for a real in-the-know experience stock up at the market and head for the Collserola hills.

Ciutadella Park

Despite its size, Spain's second city is a surprisingly easy place to find your way around. In effect, it's a series of self-contained neighbourhoods stretching out from the harbour, flanked by parks, hills and woodland. Much of what there is to see in the centre – Gothic cathedral, Picasso museum, markets, Gaudí buildings and art galleries – can be reached on foot, while a fast, cheap, integrated public transport system takes you directly to the peripheral attractions and suburbs. Meanwhile, bike tours, sightseeing buses and cruise boats all offer a different way of seeing the city.

True, for all its go-ahead feel, Barcelona has its problems, not least a petty crime rate that occasionally makes the international news. But there's no need to be unduly paranoid, and it would be a shame to stick solely to the main tourist sights as you'll miss out on so much. Tapas bars hidden down decrepit alleys, designer boutiques in gentrified Old Town quarters, street opera singers belting out an aria, bargain lunches in workers' taverns, neighbourhood funicular rides, unmarked gourmet restaurants, craft workshops, restored medieval palaces and specialist galleries all exemplify Barcelona just as much as La Rambla or Gaudí's Sagrada Família.

some of the best chefs in Europe – its late-night bars, even its football team, the mercurial, incomparable FC Barcelona. Add a spruced-up waterfront, seven kilometres of resort-standard sandy beach, and Olympic-rated sports and leisure facilities, and you have a city that entertains and cossets locals and visitors alike.

When to visit

Barcelona is an established city-break destination with a year-round tourist, business and convention trade. Different seasons have different attractions, from spring dance festivals to Christmas markets, but there's always something going on. As far as the weather is concerned, the best times to go are spring and autumn, when the temperatures are comfortably warm and walking the streets isn't a chore. In summer, the city can be very hot and humid while August sees many shops, bars and restaurants close as the locals head out of the city in droves. It's worth considering a winter break, as long as you don't mind the prospect of occasional rain. It's generally still warm enough to sit out at a café, for example, even in December or January.

Where to...

Shop

Designer and high-street fashion can be found in the Eixample along Passeig de Gràcia and Rambla de Catalunya, though for new names and boutiques the best hunting ground is in the Old Town streets around Passeig del Born (La Ribera). Second-hand and vintage clothing stores line Carrer de la Riera Baixa (El Raval), there's music and streetwear along nearby Carrer dels Tallers, and for antiques and curios it's best in the streets near Carrer Banys Nous (Barri Gòtic). The markets, meanwhile, are king, from the heavyweight Boqueria to lesser-known gems like the Mercat Santa Caterina in trendy Sant Pere or Gràcia's Mercat de la Llibertat.
OUR FAVOURITES: Artesania Catalunya, see page 40. Bulevard dels Antiquaris, see page 101. El Corte Inglés, see page 30.

Eat

In the popular Old Town areas food and service can be indifferent and expensive. There are some great bars and restaurants in tourist-heavy La Ribera and the Barri Gòtic, but you should explore the neighbourhoods of Sant Pere, El Raval and Poble Sec for the best local finds. Michelin stars and big bills are mostly found in the Eixample, while for the best fish and seafood head for harbourside Barceloneta or the Port Olímpic. The district of Gràcia is also a nice, village-like place to spend the evening, with plenty of good mid-range restaurants.
OUR FAVOURITES: Ca l'Estevet, see page 59. Bodega la Plata, see page 42. Gresca, see page 117.

Drink

The city should probably be called Bar-Celona – as whatever you're looking for, you'll find it here, from bohemian boozer to cocktail bar. Passeig del Born (La Ribera) is one of the hottest destinations, with Sant Pere hard on its heels, while there's an edgier scene in El Raval and around Carrer de Blai (Poble Sec). The main concentration of designer bars (and the city's gay scene) is in the Esquerra de l'Eixample, while the theme bars of Port Olímpic are mainstream playgrounds for locals and visitors. Bars usually stay open till any time between 11pm and 2–3am.
OUR FAVOURITES: Boadas, see page 31. Can Paixano, see page 51. Milk, see page 44

Go out

Clubs in Barcelona start late and go on until 5 or 6am, and while Thursday to Sunday sees the most action, there are DJs on the decks every night. The big-name venues tend to be in the old industrial zones like Poblenou; downtown clubs are often jazz-orientated, though local rock, pop, indie and even flamenco get regular airings in venues across the Barri Gòtic and El Raval. For typically Catalan surroundings, a classical concert at Sant Pere's Palau de la Música Catalana can't be beaten, while the principal venue in the Eixample is L'Auditori.
OUR FAVOURITES: Razzmatazz, see page 119. Bikini, see page 135. Sala Apolo, see page 89.

Barcelona at a glance

Camp Nou, Pedralbes and Sarrià-Sant Gervasi p.128.
Shops, galleries and a magnificent football stadium.

Dreta de l'Eixample p.94.
The "right-hand" side of the modern
city centre has an unparalleled displa
of modernista architecture.

Esquerra de l'Eixample p.112.
The city centre's "left-hand" side offers
cool bars, top-end restaurants and the
gay quarter.

El Raval p.52.
Up-and-coming Old Town neighbourhood.

Montjuïc p.80.
The art museums, castle and gardens
make for a popular day out.

Barri Gòtic p.32.
The "Gothic Quarter" preserves
the city's historic core.

| 0 | metres | 500 |
| 0 | yards | 500 |

Along La Rambla p.24.
Barcelona's most famous avenue.

Gràcia and Park Güell p.120.
Visit Gràcia to see Gaudí's
inspiring urban park.

Sagrada Família and Glòries p.104.
Barcelona's most amazing
building is Gaudí's unfinished
masterwork of a church.

Sant Pere p.64.
A great market plus fashionable
bars, boutiques and restaurants.

La Ribera p.68.
The medieval artisans' quarter is
home to the Picasso Museum.

Parc de la Ciutadella p.76.
A favourite park on the edge
of the Old Town.

Port Olímpic and Poblenou p.90.
Beaches, bars and urban recreation
along the city's revitalized waterfront.

Port Vell and Barceloneta p.46.
Top beaches and seafood restaurants.

15

Things not to miss

It's not possible to see everything that Barcelona has to offer in one trip – and we don't suggest you try. What follows is a selective taste of the city's highlights, from museums and galleries to restaurants and clubs. All have a page reference to take you straight into the Guide, where you can find out more.

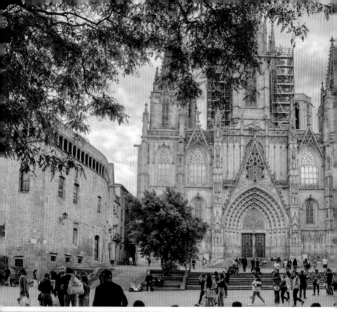

< **CaixaForum**
See page 81
There's always an exhibition worth seeing in the city's best arts and cultural centre – as well as all sorts of events.

∨ **El Xampanyet**
See page 74
Step into this La Ribera institution for a glass of Catalan fizz and a bite or two before dinner.

< La Seu
See page 32

Pride of the Gothic era, the city's majestic medieval cathedral anchors the Old Town.

∨ Compartir
See page 117

A chance to sample exquisite Mediterranean dishes created by three former *El Bulli* chefs, at this (relatively) affordable eatery in the Eixample district.

THINGS NOT TO MISS

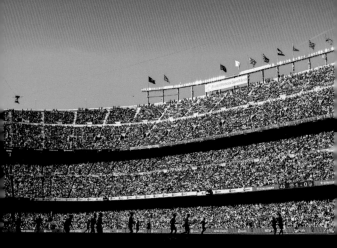

∧ Camp Nou and FC Barcelona
See page 128
Tour one of Europe's most magnificent stadiums, home to the local football heroes.

< Mercat de la Boqueria
See page 25
The city's finest food market is a show in its own right, busy with locals and tourists from dawn to dusk.

∧ Gran Teatre del Liceu
See page 28
Book ahead for opera tickets at this renowned city landmark, though the guided tours are open to all.

∨ Parc de Collserola
See page 136
Barcelona is backed by hills which are home to an impressive natural park.

∧ **City beaches**
See page 91
The great urban escape is to the city's seven kilometres of sand-fringed sea, dotted with parks and playgrounds.

< **Jardí Botànic de Barcelona**
See page 87
These impressive botanical gardens spread across a hillside above the Olympic Stadium.

< **Parc de la Ciutadella**
See page 76
Whatever the season, the city's nicest park always springs a surprise.

∨ **Port Olímpic**
See page 90
Twin towers and the landmark Frank Gehry fish dominate Barcelona's liveliest resort area.

THINGS NOT TO MISS

Day One in Barcelona

La Rambla. See page 24. Everyone starts with a stroll down Barcelona's most emblematic street.

Mercat de la Boqueria. See page 25. Wander through the stalls of one of Europe's best markets and soak up the vibrant atmosphere.

La Seu. See page 32. The calm cloister of Barcelona's cathedral is a haven amid the bustle of the Barri Gòtic.

Museu d'Història de Barcelona. See page 36. This place holds the archeological history of Roman Barcelona – right under your feet.

🍴 **Lunch.** See page 43. Stop near the church of Santa María del Pi for alfresco drinks and a market-fresh meal at *Taller de Tapas*.

Museu Picasso. See page 68. Walk through the tight-knit medieval streets of La Ribera to this must-see museum, housed in the city where Picasso developed his inimitable style.

Parc de la Ciutadella. See page 76. Take time out to stroll the gardens or row on the lake of the city's favourite park.

Port Olímpic. See page 90. The beach, boardwalk and seafront promenade set the scene for a blissful sundowner

🍴 **Dinner.** See page 60. Some of the city's hottest restaurants are in the resurgent El Raval area. Try *Suculent* for bistro classics from star chef Toni Romero.

Mercat de La Boqueria

Museu Picasso

Port Olímpic

Day Two in Barcelona

Sagrada Família. See page 104. To avoid the worst of the bustling crowds, arrive at Gaudí's masterpiece at opening time.

Passeig de Gràcia. See page 94. Europe's most extraordinary urban architecture decorates the modern city's main avenue.

Museu Egipci de Barcelona. See page 97. A captivating collection including mummies, amulets and sarcophagi transports you back to ancient Egypt.

 Lunch. See page 103. Join the queue for a spot at *Tapas 24*, where Michelin-starred chef Carles Abellán gets back to basics with simple comfort food.

Museu Nacional d'Art de Catalunya. See page 83. The triumphant landscaped approach to Montjuïc culminates in the extraordinary Catalan National Art Gallery.

Fundació Joan Miró. See page 86. The modernist building on Montjuïc houses the life's work of Catalan artist Joan Miró.

Ride the Telefèric del Port. See page 87. A thrilling cable car sweeps you across the inner harbour from Montjuïc to Port Vell.

Barceloneta. See page 48. For marina or beach views, grab a table at an outdoor café in the old fishermen's quarter.

 Dinner. See page 74. After a cold beer in up-and-coming Sant Pere, splash out on top-quality seafood at *Cal Pep*.

Sagrada Família

Telefèric del Port

W Hotel on Barceloneta beach

Modernista Barcelona

Visionary *modernista* architects, like Antoni Gaudí, changed the way people looked at buildings. Their style, a sort of Catalan Art Nouveau, left Barcelona with an extraordinary architectural legacy that goes far beyond the famous sights of the Sagrada Família church and Park Güell.

Recinte de Sant Pau. See page 105. Don't miss Lluís Domènech i Montaner's innovative public hospital, near the Sagrada Família.

La Pedrera. See page 74. Inventive design permeates every aspect of Gaudí's fantastical "stone quarry" apartment building.

Casa Amatller. See page 95. Catch a guided tour of this stunning house belonging to a nineteenth-century chocolate manufacturer.

Casa Amatller

Lunch. See page 101. Take a lunch stop at *Cafè del Centre*, a 19th-century *modernista* café.

Palau de la Música Catalana. See page 64. Book in advance for a tour of this dramatic concert hall, or buy a ticket for an evening performance.

Arc de Triomf. See page 76. Gateway to the Ciutadella park is this giant red-brick arch.

Castell dels Tres Dragons. See page 78. The eye-catching "castle" in Parc de la Ciutadella is a *modernista* delight.

Palau de la Música Catalana

Dinner. See page 122. In summer, Park Güell is open until well into the evening – and the bars and restaurants of fashionable Gràcia are close at hand.

Arc de Triomf

Budget Barcelona

Barcelona may be one of Europe's most fashionable cities, but it remains remarkably good value as far as most visitors are concerned. Here's how to eat well, see the major sights and enjoy yourself, without breaking the bank.

La Rambla. See page 24. Barcelona's greatest show – a stroll down La Rambla – is a free spectacle around the clock.

MNAC. See page 83. The ticket for the showpiece Museu Nacional d'Art de Catalunya is valid for two full days, and there's free entry on the first Sunday of every month.

Lunch. See page 42. Virtually every restaurant offers a weekday *menú del dia*, so lunch is a bargain at places like *La Sosenga*, where dinner might cost three times as much.

Museu Nacional d'Art de Catalunya

Relax at the beach. See page 91. Enjoy seven kilometres of sand, boardwalks and promenades.

Font Màgica. See page 82. There's no charge to watch this magnificent display of water and light.

CaixaForum. See page 81. Entry to this dazzling arts and cultural centre costs less than a cocktail.

CaixaForum

Parc de la Ciutadella. See page 76. Unfurl a picnic blanket in the city's green lung.

Dinner. See page 67. Many of Barcelona's markets also have stylish restaurants attached – such as *Cuines Santa Caterina* in Sant Pere's dramatic Mercat de Santa Caterina.

Rambla de Canaletes

PLACES

Sidewalk café

Along La Rambla

No day in the city seems complete without a stroll along La Rambla, Spain's most famous thoroughfare. Cutting through Barcelona's Old Town areas, and connecting Plaça de Catalunya with the harbour, it's at the heart of the city's self-image – lined with cafés, restaurants, souvenir shops, flower stalls and newspaper kiosks. The name (from the Arabic *ramla* or "sand") refers to a seasonal streambed that was paved over in medieval times. Since the nineteenth century it's been a fashionable promenade, and today the show goes on, as human statues, portrait painters, buskers and card sharps add to the vibrancy of Barcelona's most enthralling street. There are metro stops at Catalunya (top of La Rambla), Liceu (middle) and Drassanes (bottom), or you can walk the entire length in about fifteen minutes.

Plaça de Catalunya

MAP P.26, POCKET MAP D10.
Ⓜ Catalunya.

The huge formal square at the top of La Rambla stands right at the heart of the city. It's not only the focal point of events and demonstrations – notably a mass

Plaça de Catalunya

party on New Year's Eve – but also the site of prominent landmarks like the main city tourist office, the white-faced El Corte Inglés department store and El Triangle shopping centre.

La Rambla itself actually comprises five separate named sections, starting with the northern stretch, Rambla Canaletes, nearest Plaça de Catalunya, which is marked by an iron fountain – a drink from this supposedly means you'll never leave Barcelona. Further down is the sudden profusion of flower stalls on Rambla Sant Josep, near the Boqueria market. The bird market which used to be on Rambla Estudis closed down due to stricter animal protection legislation.

Església de Betlem

MAP P.26, POCKET MAP C11.
Rambla 107. Ⓜ Liceu.

It seems hard to believe, but La Rambla was a war zone during the Spanish Civil War as the city erupted into factionalism in 1937. George Orwell was caught in the

Església de Betlem

crossfire (an episode recorded in his *Homage to Catalonia*) and, with anarchists sacking the city's churches at will, the rich interior of the Baroque Església de Betlem was completely destroyed. However, the main facade on C/del Carme still sports a fine, sculpted portal.

Palau Moja

MAP P.26, POCKET MAP D11.
Rambla 188. Ⓜ Liceu. Ⓦ bit.ly/PalauMoja. Free.

The arcaded Palau Moja dates from the late eighteenth century and still retains an exterior staircase and elegant great hall. The palace's gallery (entrance is around the corner in C/Portaferrissa) is occasionally open for exhibitions relating to all things Catalan. Take a look at the illustrated tiles above the fountain at the start of C/de la Portaferrissa, showing the medieval gate (the Porta Ferriça) and market once sited here.

Palau de la Virreina

MAP P.26, POCKET MAP C12.
Rambla 99. Ⓜ Liceu. Ⓦ bit.ly/PalauVirreina. Free.

Graceful eighteenth-century Palau de la Virreina is the HQ of the cultural department of the Ajuntament (city council), and there's a ground-floor information centre where you can find out about upcoming events and buy tickets (also more information on their website). Various galleries and studios house changing exhibitions of contemporary art and photography, while at the back of the palace courtyard you can usually see the city's enormous Carnival giants (*gegants*), representing the thirteenth-century Catalan king Jaume I and his wife Violant. The origin of these ornate, five-metre-high figures is unclear, though they probably first enlivened medieval travelling fairs and are now an integral part of Barcelona's festival parades.

Mercat de la Boqueria

MAP P.26, POCKET MAP C12.
Rambla 91. Ⓜ Liceu. Ⓦ boqueria.info. Free.

Other markets might protest, but the city's glorious main food market really can claim to be the best in Spain. It's officially called

Along La Rambla

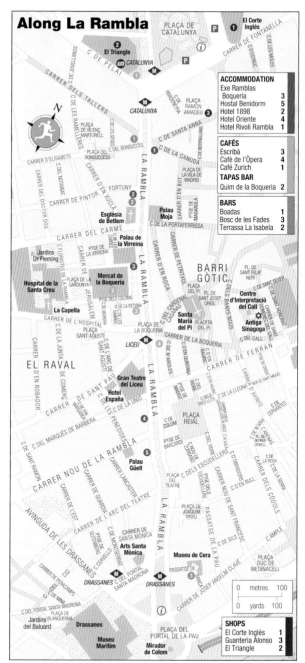

ACCOMMODATION

Exe Ramblas Boqueria	3
Hostal Benidorm	5
Hotel 1898	2
Hotel Oriente	4
Hotel Rivoli Rambla	1

CAFÉS

Escribà	3
Cafè de l'Òpera	4
Café Zurich	1

TAPAS BAR

Quim de la Boqueria	2

BARS

Boadas	1
Bosc de les Fades	3
Terrassa La Isabela	2

SHOPS

El Corte Inglés	1
Guanteria Alonso	3
El Triangle	2

Mercat de la Boqueria

the Mercat Sant Josep, though everyone knows it as La Boqueria. A riot of noise and colour, it's as popular with locals who come here to shop daily as with snap-happy tourists. Everything radiates out from the central fish and seafood stalls – bunches of herbs, pots of spices, baskets of wild mushrooms, mounds of cheese and sausage, racks of bread, hanging hams and overloaded meat counters. It's easy to get waylaid at the entrance by the fruit cartons and squeezed juices, but the flagship fruit and veg stalls here are pricey. It's better value further in, in particular in the small outdoor square just beyond the north side of the market where the local allotment holders and market-gardeners gather. Everyone has a favourite market stall, but don't miss Petras and its array of wild mushrooms (it's at the back), or Frutas y Verduras Jesús y Carmen, which is framed with colourful bundles of exotic chillies. And of course, there are some excellent stand-up tapas bars in the market as well, open from dawn onward for the traders.

Plaça de la Boqueria
MAP P.26, POCKET MAP C12.
Ⓜ Liceu.
The halfway point of La Rambla is marked by Plaça de la Boqueria,

An insider's guide to La Rambla

There are pavement cafés and restaurants all the way down La Rambla, but the food can be indifferent and the prices high, so be warned. (For better value, go into the Boqueria market, where the traders eat.) The strolling crowds, too, provide perfect cover for pickpockets – keep a wary eye on your possessions at all times, especially when watching the buskers or shopping at the kiosks. And – however easy it looks to win – if you're going to play cards or dice with a man on a street, you've only yourself to blame if you get ripped off.

Gran Teatre del Liceu

MAP P.26, POCKET MAP C13.
Rambla 51–59. Ⓜ Liceu.
Ⓦ liceubarcelona.cat. Charge.

Barcelona's celebrated opera house was first founded in 1847 and rebuilt after a fire in 1861 to become Spain's grandest theatre. Regarded as a bastion of the city's late nineteenth-century commercial and intellectual classes, the Liceu was devastated again in 1893 when an anarchist threw two bombs into the stalls during a production of *William Tell* – twenty people died. It then burned down for the third time in 1994, when a workman's blowtorch set fire to the scenery of an opera set. The latest restoration of the lavishly decorated interior took five years, and the opera house opened again in 1999, complete with a modern extension, the Espai Liceu, which also houses a music and gift shop and a café. You'll see and learn most on the more expensive, hour-long 10am guided tour (the other, shorter, cheaper tours are self-guided). Highlights include the Salon of Mirrors and the impressive gilded auditorium containing almost 2300 seats, making it one of the world's largest opera houses. Some tours also include the option of visiting the glorious *modernista*-styled rooms of the Cercle del Liceu, the opera house's private members' club.

Gran Teatre del Liceu

with its large round pavement **mosaic by Joan Miró**. It's become something of a symbol for the city and is one of a number of public works in Barcelona by the artist, who was born just a couple of minutes away in the Barri Gòtic. Over at Rambla 82, **Casa Bruno Quadros** – the lower floor is now the Caixa Sabadell – was built in the 1890s to house an umbrella store, which explains its delightful facade, decorated with Oriental designs, dragons and parasols.

La Rambla statues

Time stands still for no man – not even for the famed human statues of La Rambla, who make a living out of doing just that. A motley crew of figures once flanked the length of the street, but change is inevitable, and in an effort to keep pedestrian traffic moving, and prevent pickpockets from preying on the gathering crowds, the city has moved the human statues to the wide stretch of Rambla de Santa Mònica. The number of statues has also been capped at thirty a year, with performers being required to audition for the permit-only slots. Despite the cutback in territory and number, the remaining human statues are still an attraction. Be it Galileo or a horned demon, these stalwarts of La Rambla continue to climb upon their plinths and strike a pose. What else is a statue going to do?

For Liceu performances, check the website for details and make bookings well in advance. The traditional meeting place for audience and performers alike, meanwhile, is the famous *Café de l'Òpera*, just across La Rambla.

Arts Santa Mònica

MAP P.26, POCKET MAP C14.
Rambla 7. Ⓜ Drassanes.
Ⓦ artssantamonica.gencat.cat. Free.

Down from the Liceu, the bottom part of La Rambla (Rambla de Santa Mònica) was historically a theatre and red-light district, and it still has a rough edge or two. Flagship building is the Augustinian convent of Santa Mònica, which dates originally from 1626, making it the oldest building on La Rambla. It was remodelled in the 1980s as a contemporary arts centre, and hosts regularly changing exhibitions – it's an unusual gallery space dedicated to "artistic creation, science, thought and communication" so there's usually something worth seeing, from an offbeat art installation to a show of archive photographs. Meanwhile,

pavement artists and palm readers set up stalls outside on La Rambla, augmented on weekend afternoons by a street market selling jewellery, beads, bags and ornaments.

Museu de Cera

MAP P.26, POCKET MAP C14.
Rambla 4–6, entrance on Ptge. de Banca.
Ⓜ Drassanes. Ⓦ museocerabcn.com.
Charge.

You'd have to be hard-hearted indeed not to derive some pleasure from the city's wax museum. Located in a nineteenth-century bank building, it presents an ever more ludicrous series of tableaux in cavernous salons and gloomy corridors, depicting recitals, meetings and parlour gatherings attended by an anachronistic – not to say perverse – collection of characters, from Jack Sparrow to Chewbacca. Needless to say, it's enormously amusing, culminating in cheesy underwater tunnels and space capsules and an unpleasant "Terror Room". Even if this doesn't appeal, it is definitely worth poking your head into the museum's extraordinary grotto bar, the *Bosc de les Fades*.

ALONG LA RAMBLA

Museum of Wax Barcelona

Shops

El Corte Inglés

MAP P.26, POCKET MAP E10.
Pl. de Catalunya 14. Ⓜ Catalunya.
Ⓦ elcorteingles.es.

The city's biggest department store has nine retail floors (fashion, cosmetics, household goods, toys), a good basement supermarket, and – best of all – a top-floor café with terrific views. For music, books, computers and sports gear, head for the nearby branch at Av. Portal de l'Àngel 19.

Guanteria Alonso

MAP P.26, POCKET MAP D11.
C/de Santa Anna 27. Ⓜ Liceu.
Ⓦ guanteria-alonso.com.

An emblematic Gòtic shop, resplendent with its wooden *modernista* facade since 1973. The speciality is beautifully soft gloves for men and women, and a huge range of fans. You'll also find handkerchiefs, shawls and veils.

El Triangle

MAP P.26, POCKET MAP D10.
Pl. de Catalunya 4. Ⓜ Catalunya.
Ⓦ eltriangle.es.

Shopping centre dominated by the flagship FNAC store, which specializes in books (good English-language selection), music, film and computer stuff. Also a Camper (for shoes), Massimo Dutti (fashion) and Sephora (cosmetics), plus lots of boutiques, and a café on the ground floor.

Cafés

Escribà

MAP P.26, POCKET MAP C12.
Rambla 83. Ⓜ Liceu. Ⓦ escriba.es.

Wonderful pastries and cakes from the renowned Escribà family business in a classy *modernista* shop. Many rate this as the best patisserie in Barcelona. €

Cafè de l'Òpera

MAP P.26, POCKET MAP C12.

Escribà

Rambla 74. Ⓜ **Liceu.**
Ⓦ **cafeoperabcn.com.**
If you're going to pay through the nose for a seat on La Rambla, it may as well be at this famous old café-bar opposite the opera house, which retains a *fin-de-siècle* feel. Surprisingly, it's not a complete tourist-fest and locals pop in day and night for drinks, cakes and tapas. €

Café Zurich
MAP P.26, POCKET MAP D10.
Pl. Catalunya 1. Ⓜ **Catalunya.**
Ⓦ **facebook.com/cafezurichdebarcelona.**
The most famous meet-and-greet café in town, right at the top of La Rambla and underneath El Triangle shopping centre. It's good for drinks, less so for food. There's a huge pavement terrace, but sit inside if you don't want to be bothered by endless rounds of buskers and beggars. €

Restaurant and tapas bar

Quim de la Boqueria
MAP P.26, POCKET MAP C12.
Mercat de la Boqueria, La Rambla 91.
Ⓜ **Catalunya.** Ⓦ **elquimdelaboqueria.com.**
The beating heart of the Boqueria market is this superb tapas bar. The house speciality is fried eggs with various gourmet options: baby squid, wild mushrooms, prawns cooked in cava and many more. You'll also find oxtail stew, sausage with beans and various other local dishes. Arrive early for a seat at the bar. €€

Bars

Boadas
MAP P.26, POCKET MAP D11.
C/dels Tallers 1. Ⓜ **Catalunya.**
Ⓦ **boadascocktails.com.**
Inside Barcelona's oldest cocktail bar, tuxedoed bartenders shake,

Bosc de les Fades

stir and pour classic drinks for a well-dressed crowd against an Art Deco background. It's a timeless place that's a perfect start for a sophisticated night on the town.

Bosc de les Fades
MAP P.26, POCKET MAP C14.
Ptge. de Banca. 5 Ⓜ **Drassanes.**
Ⓦ **boscdelesfades.com.**
Down an alley by the wax museum, the "Forest of the Fairies" is festooned with gnarled plaster tree trunks, hanging branches, fountains and stalactites. It's a bit cheesy, which is perhaps why it's a huge hit with the twenty-something crowd who huddle in the grottoes with a cocktail or two.

Terrassa La Isabela
MAP P.26, POCKET MAP C5.
Rambla 109. Ⓜ **Liceu.**
Ⓦ **terraza-laisabela.com.**
Get a bird's-eye look at La Rambla from *Hotel 1898*'s stylish rooftop terrace bar. The food and cocktails aren't cheap, but the views are priceless.

Barri Gòtic

The Barri Gòtic, or Gothic Quarter, on the east side of La Rambla, forms the heart of Barcelona's Old Town. Its buildings date principally from the fourteenth and fifteenth centuries, and culminate in the extraordinary Gothic cathedral known as La Seu. Around here are hidden squares, some fascinating museums, the city's old Jewish quarter and the remains of the Roman walls. It takes the best part of a day to see everything – longer if you factor in the abundant cafés, antique shops, boutiques and galleries. Note that the southern area, en route to the harbour, is rather less gentrified than the cathedral district – take care at night in the poorly lit streets. Metro stations Liceu (west), Jaume I (east) and Drassanes (south) provide access to the neighbourhood.

La Seu

MAP P.34, POCKET MAP E12.
Pl. de la Seu. Ⓜ Jaume I.
Ⓦ catedralbcn.org. Free during general admission times, otherwise charge.
Barcelona's cathedral is one of the great Gothic buildings of Spain, dedicated to Santa Eulàlia, who was martyred by the Romans for daring to prefer Christianity – her ornate tomb rests in a crypt beneath the high altar. A magnificent fourteenth-century **cloister** looks over a lush tropical garden complete with soaring palm trees and honking white geese. There's also glittering church treasure on show in the cathedral museum.

Performances of the Catalan national dance, the *sardana*, take

La Seu

place in front of the cathedral (usually Sun at noon, plus Easter–Nov Sat at 6pm), while the pedestrianized Avinguda de la Catedral hosts an antiques market every Thursday, and a Christmas craft fair in December.

Museu Diocesà

MAP P.34, POCKET MAP E12.
Av. Catedral 4. Ⓜ Jaume I. Ⓦ bit.ly/Diocesa. Charge.
Stand back to look at the cathedral buildings and it's easy to see the line of Roman towers that originally stood on this spot incorporated into the later medieval structures. One such tower formed part of the cathedral almshouse, now the Museu Diocesà, whose soaring spaces have been beautifully adapted to show an impressive collection of religious art and church treasures. The ticket also includes entrance into the temporary art and architecture exhibitions held here.

Reial Cercle Artístic

MAP P.34, POCKET MAP D12.
C/Arcs 5. Ⓜ Jaume I.
Ⓦ reialcercleartistic.cat. Charge.
The handsome Gothic palace housing the Royal Art Circle hosts various free exhibitions and concerts, though the big draw is the collection of 44 original sculptures by Salvador Dalí, completed in the 1970s. A lovely terrace restaurant above the Gothic streets also offers a pricey lunch, while on your way to or from the cathedral spare a glance for the graffiti-like frieze surmounting the nearby **Collegi d'Arquitectes** on Plaça Nova – designed by that other inimitable master, Pablo Picasso.

Plaça del Rei

MAP P.34, POCKET MAP E12.
Ⓜ Jaume I.
The harmonious enclosed square of Plaça del Rei was once the palace courtyard of the Counts of Barcelona. Stairs climb from

Plaça Reial

here to the palace's main hall, the fourteenth-century **Saló del Tinell**. It was here that Ferdinand and Isabella received Christopher Columbus on his triumphant return from his famous voyage of 1492. At one time the Spanish Inquisition met in the hall, taking full advantage of the popular belief that the walls would move if a lie was spoken. Nowadays it hosts temporary exhibitions, while concerts are occasionally held in the hall or outside in the square. The palace buildings include the beautiful fourteenth-century **Capella de Santa Àgata**, and the romantic Renaissance **Torre del Rei Martí**. There's no public access to the tower, but the interiors of the hall and chapel can usually be seen during a visit to the adjacent Museu d'Història de Barcelona.

Museu Frederic Marès

MAP P.34, POCKET MAP E12.
Pl. de Sant Iu 5–6. Ⓜ Jaume I.
Ⓦ museumares.bcn.cat. Charge, free Sun after 3pm & first Sun of the month.
Don't miss a visit to one of the Old Town's most fascinating museums, which occupies a wing

34

BARRI GÒTIC

Barri Gòtic

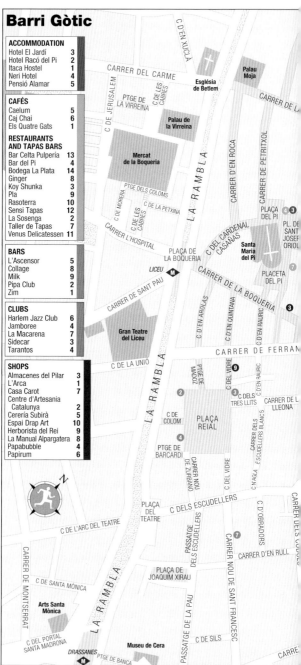

ACCOMMODATION
Hotel El Jardí	3
Hotel Racó del Pi	2
Itaca Hostel	1
Neri Hotel	4
Pensió Alamar	5

CAFÉS
Caelum	5
Caj Chai	6
Els Quatre Gats	1

RESTAURANTS AND TAPAS BARS
Bar Celta Pulpería	13
Bar del Pi	4
Bodega La Plata	14
Ginger	8
Koy Shunka	3
Pla	9
Rasoterra	10
Sensi Tapas	12
La Sosenga	2
Taller de Tapas	7
Venus Delicatessen	11

BARS
L'Ascensor	5
Collage	8
Milk	9
Pipa Club	2
Zim	1

CLUBS
Harlem Jazz Club	6
Jamboree	4
La Macarena	7
Sidecar	3
Tarantos	4

SHOPS
Almacenes del Pilar	3
L'Arca	1
Casa Carot	7
Centre d'Artesania Catalunya	2
Cerería Subirà	5
Espai Drap Art	10
Herborista del Rei	9
La Manual Alpargatera	8
Papabubble	4
Papirum	6

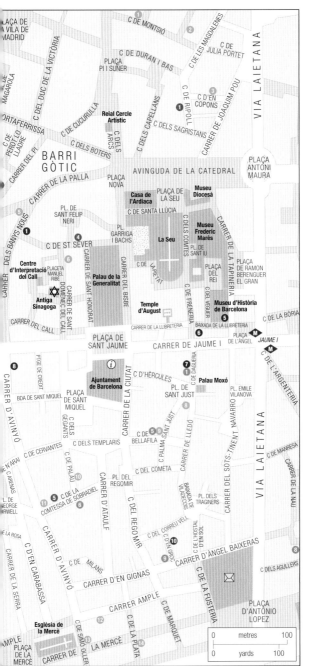

PLAÇA DE LA VILA DE MADRID

C DE MONTSIÓ ①②

C DE LES MAGDALENES

C DE JULIA PORTET

VIA LAIETANA

C DE DURAN I BAS

PLAÇA PI I SUÑER

C D'EN COPONS ③

C DE RIPOLL ①

C DE JOAQUIM POU

C DEL DUC DE LA VICTÒRIA

CASA DE MAGAROLA

C DE PEROT LO LLADRE

PORTAFERRISSA

C DE CUCURULLA

Reial Cercle Artístic

C DELS CAPELLANS

C DELS ARCS

C DELS SAGRISTANS

C DELS BOTERS

BARRI GÒTIC

CARRER DEL PI

CARRER DE LA PALLA

PLAÇA NOVA

AVINGUDA DE LA CATEDRAL

PLAÇA ANTONI MAURA

Casa de l'Ardiaca

PLAÇA DE LA SEU

Museu Diocesà

PL. DE SANT FELIP NERI

C DE SANTA LLÚCIA

C DELS BANYS NOUS ⑤①

C DE ST SEVER

PL. GARRIGA I BACHS

Museu Frederic Marès

CARRER DE LA TAPINERIA

Centre d'Interpretació del Call ⑥

PLACETA MANUEL RIBÉ

La Seu

C DELS COMTES

PL. DE SANT IU

PLAÇA DE RAMON BERENGUER EL GRAN

Palau de la Generalitat ④

CARRER DE SANT HONORAT

CARRER DEL BISBE

C DE VAPIETAT

PLAÇA DEL REI

✡ Antiga Sinagoga

CARRER DE SANT DOMÈNEC DEL CALL

Temple d'August

C DE FRENERIA

Museu d'Història de Barcelona ⑥

CARRER DEL CALL

CARRER DE LA LLIBRETERIA

C DEL VEGUER

C DE LA BÒRIA

PLAÇA DE SANT JAUME

BAIXADA DE LA LLIBRETERIA

PLAÇA DE L'ÀNGEL Ⓜ JAUME I

CARRER DE JAUME I

Ⓜ

ⓘ Ajuntament de Barcelona

C D'HÈRCULES ⑦①

C DE L'ARGENTERIA

C DE DAGUERIA

Palau Moxó

PIGE DE CREDIT

PLAÇA DE SANT MIQUEL

PL. DE SANT JUST

PL. EMILE VILANOVA

BDA DE SANT MIQUEL

CARRER DE LA CIUTAT

CARRER DELS SOTS-TINENT NAVARRO

CARRER D'AVINYÓ ⑧

C DELS GEGANTS

C DELS TEMPLARIS

C DE SANT JUST ⑧

C DE LLEDÓ

C DE LA BELLAFILA ⑤⑩

C PALMA SANT JUST

VIA LAIETANA

C DE MANRESA

C DE CERVANTES

C DEL COMETA

CARRER DE LA NAU

C N'ARAI

C DE PALAU ⑩

PL. DEL REGOMIR

BAIXADA DE VILADECOLS

PL. DELS TRAGINERS

C DE ARENAS

PL. DE GEORGE ORWELL

C DE LA COMTESSA DE SOBRADIEL ⑤⑥①

CARRER D'ATAÜLF

C DEL REGOMIR

C DEL CORREU VELL

C DE LA ROSA

C EN GROC ⑩

C DELS AGULLERS ⑧

CARRER D'EN AVINYÓ

C DE MILANS

C DEL HOSTAL D'EN SOL

CARRER D'ÀNGEL BAIXERAS

CARRER DE LA FUSTERIA

C DE LA SERRA

CARRER D'EN GIGNAS

PLAÇA D'ANTÓNIO LOPEZ

CARRER DE LA CARABASSA

CARRER AMPLE ⑫

C DE MARQUET

C DE LA PLATA

Església de la Mercè

C DE SIMÓ OLLER ⑬

LA MERCÈ ⑭

PLAÇA DE LA MERCÈ

CARRER AMPLE

AMPLE

| 0 | metres | 100 |
| 0 | yards | 100 |

of the old royal palace. It celebrates the diverse passions of sculptor, painter and restorer Frederic Marès (1893–1991), whose beautifully presented collection of ancient and medieval sculpture does little to prepare visitors for Marès' true obsession, namely a kaleidoscopic array of curios and collectibles. Entire rooms are devoted to keys and locks, cigarette cards and snuffboxes, fans, gloves and brooches, walking sticks, dolls' houses, old gramophones and archaic bicycles – to list just a sample of what's in the collection.

Museu d'Història de Barcelona (MUHBA)

MAP P.34, POCKET MAP E12.
Pl. del Rei, entrance on C/del Veguer.
Ⓜ Jaume l. Ⓦ museuhistoria.bcn.cat.
Charge.
The Barcelona History Museum comprises half a dozen sites across the city, though its principal hub is what's known as the "Conjunt Monumental" (or monumental ensemble) of Plaça del Rei, whose crucial draw is an amazing

underground archeological section – nothing less than the remains of the Roman city of Barcino (first century BC to the sixth century AD), which stretch under the surrounding streets as far as the cathedral. Excavations and explanatory diagrams show the full extent of the streets and buildings – from lookout towers to laundries – while models, mosaics, murals and finds help flesh out the reality of daily life in Barcino.

There's a well-stocked book and gift shop on site (entrance on C/Llibreteria), while the museum ticket also allows entry to the other MUHBA sites, notably the Poble Sec air-raid shelter and Pedralbes monastery.

Església de Santa María del Pi

MAP P.34, POCKET MAP D12.
Pl. Sant Josep Oriol. Ⓜ Liceu.
Ⓦ basilicadelpi.cat. Charge.
The fourteenth-century church of Santa María is known for its marvellous stained glass, particularly a 10m-wide rose

Temple d'August de Barcelona

window (often claimed, rather boldly, to be the largest in the world). The church flanks Plaça Sant Josep Oriol, the prettiest of three delightful adjacent squares and an ideal place for an outdoor coffee and a browse around the weekend **artists' market** (Sat 11am–8pm, Sun 11am–2pm).

The church is named after the pine tree that once stood here. A **farmers' market** spills across Plaça del Pi on the first and third Friday, Saturday and Sunday of the month, while the characteristic cafés of narrow **Carrer de Petritxol** (off Plaça del Pi) are the places to head to for a cup of hot chocolate – *Dulcinea* at no. 2 is the traditional choice – and a browse around the street's commercial art galleries. The most famous is **Sala Parés** at C/Petritxol 5, known as the site of Picasso's first solo exhibition.

Temple d'August de Barcelona

MAP P.34, POCKET MAP D1.
Centre Excursionista de Catalunya, C/Paradis 10. Ⓜ Jaume I.
Ⓦ bit.ly/TempleAugust. Free.
Four impressive Roman columns and the architrave of a temple dedicated to the Emperor Augustus make an incongruous spectacle, tucked away in the green-painted interior courtyard of the Centre Excursionista de Catalunya (Catalan Hiking Club). Some of the oldest constructions in Barcelona, they managed to remain intact despite medieval buildings rising up around them.

Antiga Sinagoga

MAP P.34, POCKET MAP D12.
C/Marlet 5, corner with C/Sant Domènec del Call. Ⓜ Liceu. Ⓦ sinagogamayor.com. Charge.
Barcelona's medieval Jewish quarter was centred on Calle Sant Domènec del Call, where a synagogue existed from as early as the third century AD until the pogrom of 1391, but even after

that date the building survived in various guises and has now been sympathetically restored. The city authorities have signposted a few other points of interest in what's known as "El Call Major", including the **Centre d'Interpretació del Call** in nearby Plaçeta Manuel Ribé (free), whose informative storyboards (in English) shed more light on Barcelona's fascinating Jewish heritage.

Casa de l'Ardiaca

MAP P.34, POCKET MAP E12.
C/Santa Llúcia 3. Ⓜ Jaume I.
Ⓦ bit.ly/Ardiaca. Free.
Originally the residence of the archdeacon of La Seu cathedral, this fourteenth-century house encloses a tiny cloistered and tiled courtyard, renovated by *modernista* architect Lluís Domènech i Montaner. It's now used for changing temporary exhibitions and the city's historical archives.

Palau de la Generalitat

MAP P.34, POCKET MAP D12/13.
Pl. de Sant Jaume. Ⓜ Jaume I.
Ⓦ bit.ly/PalauGen. Free.
The home of the Catalan government presents its oldest aspect around the side, where the fifteenth-century C/del Bisbe facade contains a medallion portraying Sant Jordi (St George, patron saint of Catalunya). Inside, there's a beautiful first-floor cloister, the intricately worked chapel and salon of Sant Jordi as well as an upper courtyard planted with orange trees. You can visit the interior on a one-hour guided tour on alternate weekends (Saturday and Sunday, except for August, only one or two tours each day are in English), while the Generalitat is also open on public holidays, particularly April 23 – the **Dia de Sant Jordi** (St George's Day). A nationalist holiday in Catalunya, this is also a local Valentine's Day, when it's traditional to exchange

Palau de la Generalitat

books and roses. ID such as a passport is required.

Plaça de Sant Jaume

MAP P.34, POCKET MAP D13.
Ⓜ Jaume I.

The spacious square at the end of the main Carrer de Ferran is at the heart of city and regional government business, and the traditional place for demonstrations and local festivals. Whistle-happy local police try to keep things moving, while taxis and bike-tour groups weave among the pedestrians.

Ajuntament de Barcelona

MAP P.34, POCKET MAP D13.
Pl. de Sant Jaume, entrance on C/Font de Sant Miquel. Ⓜ Jaume I. Ⓦ bit.ly/AjunBarc.
Free.

On the south side of Plaça de Sant Jaume stands Barcelona's city hall. On Sundays you're allowed into the building for a guided (in English at 10am) or self-guided tour around the splendid marble galleries and staircases. The highlights are the magnificent fourteenth-century council chamber, known as the **Saló de Cent**, and the dramatic

historical murals in the **Saló de les Cròniques** (Hall of Chronicles).

Palau Moxó

MAP P.34, POCKET MAP E13.
Pl. de Sant Just 4. Ⓜ Jaume I.
Ⓦ palaumoxobcn.blogspot.com. Charge.
The Palau Moxó has been in the hands of the same family since 1770, which makes it unique in Barcelona – especially since most other palatial Baroque residences were destroyed during the Civil War. You'll see grand salons and intimate chambers on the guided tours (must be reserved in advance, see the website), while regular concerts provide another taste of the noble life.

Plaça Reial

MAP P.34, POCKET MAP C13.
Ⓜ Liceu.

The elegant Plaça Reial – hidden behind an archway off La Rambla – is studded with palm trees and decorated iron lamps (designed by the young Antoni Gaudí), and bordered by pastel-coloured arcaded buildings. Sitting in the square certainly puts you in mixed company – buskers, eccentrics, tramps and bemused visitors – though most of the really unsavoury characters have been driven off over the years and predatory waiters are usually the biggest nuisance these days. Don't expect to see too many locals until night falls, when the surrounding bars come into their own. Passing through on a Sunday morning, look in on the **coin and stamp market**.

Carrer d'Avinyó

MAP P.34, POCKET MAP D13/14.
Ⓜ **Liceu.**

Carrer d'Avinyó, running south from Carrer de Ferran towards the harbour, cuts through the most atmospheric part of the southern Barri Gòtic. Formerly a red-light district, it still looks the part – lined with dark overhanging buildings – but the funky cafés, streetwear shops and boutiques tell the story of its creeping gentrification. A few rough edges still show, particularly around **Plaça George Orwell**, a favoured hangout for locals with its cheap cafés, restaurants and bars, some of which offer seating on the lively square.

La Mercè

MAP P.34, POCKET MAP D14.
Ⓜ **Drassanes.**

In the eighteenth century, the harbourside neighbourhood known as La Mercè was home to the nobles and merchants enriched by Barcelona's maritime trade. Most moved north to the more fashionable Eixample later in the nineteenth century, and since then Carrer de la Mercè and surrounding streets (particularly Ample, d'en Gignàs and Regomir) have been home to a series of old-style taverns known as *tascas* or *bodegas* – a glass of wine from the barrel and a plate of tapas here is one of the Old Town's more authentic experiences.

At Plaça de la Mercè, the **Església de la Mercè** is the focus of the city's biggest annual bash, the Festes de la Mercè every September, dedicated to the co-patroness of Barcelona, whose image is paraded from the church. It's an excuse for a week of partying, parades, special events and concerts, culminating in spectacular pyrotechnics along the seafront.

Església de la Mercè

Shops

Almacenes del Pilar

MAP P.34, POCKET MAP D13.
C/Boqueria 43. Ⓜ Liceu. Ⓦ adelpilar.com.
A world of frills, lace, cloth and material used in the making of Spain's traditional regional costumes. You can pick up a decorated fan for just a few euros, though quality items go for a lot more.

L'Arca

MAP P.34, POCKET MAP D12.
C/Banys Nous 20. Ⓜ Liceu. Ⓦ larca.es.
Catalan brides used to fill up their nuptial trunk (*l'arca*) with embroidered linen and lace, and this shop is a treasure-trove of vintage and antique textiles. Period costumes can be hired or purchased as well – one of Kate Winslet's *Titanic* costumes came from here.

Casa Carot

MAP P.34, POCKET MAP E13.
C/Dagueria 16. Ⓜ Jaume I.
Ⓦ instagram.com/casacarot.
Set in an old dairy building, Casa Carot sells a variety of farmhouse cheeses from independent producers around Catalunya, focusing on small producers and those that guarantee the best animal welfare.

Centre d'Artesania Catalunya

MAP P.34, POCKET MAP D12.
C/Banys Nous 11. Ⓜ Liceu.
Ⓦ bit.ly/CentreArtesania.
It's always worth a look in the showroom of the arts and crafts promotion board. Exhibitions change but most of the work is contemporary in style, from basketwork to glassware, though traditional methods are still very much encouraged.

Cerería Subirà

MAP P.34, POCKET MAP E13.
Bxda. Llibreteria 7. Ⓜ Jaume I.
Ⓦ cereriasubira.cat.
Barcelona's oldest shop (it's been here since 1760) boasts a beautiful interior, selling unique handcrafted candles.

Espai Drap Art

MAP P.34, POCKET MAP E14.
C/Groc 1. Ⓜ Jaume I. Ⓦ drapart.org.

L'Arca

The Drap Art creative recycling organization has a shop and exhibition space for artists to show their wildly inventive wares, from trash bangles to tin bags.

Herboristeria del Rei

MAP P.34, POCKET MAP D13.
C/del Vidre 1. Ⓜ Liceu.
Ⓦ herboristeriadelrei.com.
A renowned, early nineteenth-century herbalist's shop, tucked off Plaça Reial, which stocks more than 250 medicinal herbs designed to combat all complaints.

La Manual Alpargatera

MAP P.34, POCKET MAP D13.
C/d'Avinyó 7. Ⓜ Liceu. Ⓦ lamanual.com.
In this traditional workshop they make and sell *alpargatas* (espadrilles) to order, as well as producing other straw, rope and basket work.

Papabubble

MAP P.34, POCKET MAP D13.
C/dels Banys Nous 3. Ⓜ Jaume I.
Ⓦ papabubble.com.
Groovy young things roll out home-made candy to a chill-out soundtrack. Come and watch them at work, sample a sweet, and take home a gorgeously wrapped gift.

Papirum

MAP P.34, POCKET MAP E13.
Baixada de la Llibreteria 2. Ⓜ Jaume I.
Ⓦ facebook.com/PapirvmBCN.
Opened in 1981, Papirum caters to notebook and ink pen enthusiasts, with divine handprinted paper, leatherbound journals, ink wells and pens of every type. It's difficult to find a classier souvenir for the people back home.

Cafés

Caelum

MAP P.34, POCKET MAP D12.
C/Palla 8. Ⓜ Liceu.
Ⓦ caelumbarcelona.com.

Caelum

The lovingly packaged confections in this upscale café-patisserie (the name is Latin for "heaven") are made in convents and monasteries across Spain. Choose from marzipan sweets from Seville, Benedictine preserves or Cistercian cookies. €

Caj Chai

MAP P.34, POCKET MAP D12.
C/Sant Domènec del Call 12. Ⓜ Liceu.
Ⓦ cajchai.com.
This refined backstreet boudoir offers a menu of painstakingly prepared teas, from Moroccan mint to organic Nepalese oolong, plus brownies, baklava and sandwiches. €

Els Quatre Gats

MAP P.34, POCKET MAP E11.
C/Montsió 3. Ⓜ Liceu. Ⓦ 4gats.com.
An absolute gem on the *modernista* route, *Els Quatre Gats* is also a nice place for a coffee and croissant, sitting at one of the tables where Picasso hung out with his artist friends back in the day. There is an adjoining restaurant, but the food is not quite at the level of its surroundings. €

Cerería Subirà candle shop

Restaurants and tapas bars

Bar Celta Pulpería

MAP P.34, POCKET MAP D14.
C/de la Mercè 16. Ⓜ Drassanes.
Ⓦ barcelta.com.
This brightly lit, no-nonsense
Galician tapas bar specializes in
dishes like *pop gallego* (octopus)
and fried green *pimientos*
(peppers), washed down with
heady regional wine. Eat at the
U-shaped bar or at tables in the
back room, and while it's not one
for a long, lazy meal, it's just right
to kick off a bout of bar-hopping.
There is a spinoff on Carrer de la
Princesa 50. €

Bar del Pi

MAP P.34, POCKET MAP D12.
Pl. Sant Josep Oriol 1. Ⓜ Liceu.
Ⓦ bardelpi.com.
Best known for its terrace tables on
one of Barcelona's prettiest squares.
Linger over drinks and sandwiches
as the Old Town reveals its charms,
especially during the weekend
artists' market. €

Bodega La Plata

MAP P.34, POCKET MAP E14.
C/de la Mercè 28. Ⓜ Drassanes.
Ⓦ barlaplata.com.
A classic taste of the Old Town,
with a marble tapas counter open
to the street (anchovies are the
speciality) and dirt-cheap wine
straight from the barrel. €

Ginger

MAP P.34, POCKET MAP E13.
C/Palma de Sant Just 1. Ⓜ Jaume I.
Ⓦ instagram.com/gingerbarbcn.
Cocktails and wines in a slickly
updated 1970s-style setting. There's
a short list of tapas ranging from
the simple (*patatas bravas* and
padrón peppers) to the elaborate
(smoked sardines with avocado and
tomato confit). €€

Koy Shunka

MAP P.34, POCKET MAP E12.
C/d'en Copons 7 Ⓜ Jaume I
Ⓦ koyshunka.com.
The city's hottest Japanese chef,
Hideki Matsuhisa, has branched out
from his original *Shunka* restaurant
with a rather more hip, nearby
sister joint, where peerless sushi
and dishes like grilled Wagyu beef

and roast black cod await. With the pricey tasting menus, it's a more rarefied experience all round, and you'll definitely need to book. €€€€

Pla

MAP P.34, POCKET MAP E13.
C/Bellafilla 5. Ⓜ Jaume I.
Ⓦ restaurantpla.cat

Cosy, candlelit and romantic, *Pla* is usually filled with twinkle-eyed couples enjoying creative international dishes. Sister restaurant *Bar del Pla* (C/Montcada 2) is a top choice for traditional tapas with subtle imaginative twists. €€€

Rasoterra

MAP P.34, POCKET MAP D13.
C/Palau 5. Ⓜ Jaume I. Ⓦ rasoterra.cat.

Plant-based diets don't have to be boring, and this lovely bistro has some ingenious recipes to prove it. The vegan and vegetarian options are far from routine, including glazed white asparagus with miso, figs and walnuts, and cavatelli with creamy courgette and pepper sauce. *Rasoterra* supports the Slow Food movement, so if you're looking for a place to chill while enjoying some exciting and new tastes – this is where you need to go. €€

Sensi Tapas

MAP P.34, POCKET MAP D14.
C/Ample 26. Ⓜ Jaume I. Ⓦ sensi.es.

Best to make reservations as this intimate space in stone and dark wood and splashes of red quickly fills with diners looking for tapas with an exotic spin. There are impeccably executed classics like buttery *patatas bravas*, but the stars of the show, such as the tender Iberian pork *tataki*, take their cues from further afield. €€

La Sosenga

MAP P.34, POCKET MAP E11.
C/de n'Amargós 1. Ⓜ Liceu. Ⓦ lasosenga.cat.

With recipes based on those in the *Llibre del Sent Sovi*, the prototype medieval Catalan cookbook, *La Sosenga* is a welcoming change from the tourist-oriented restaurants that have taken over much of the Barri Gòtic. There's a good fixed-price lunch too. €€

Taller de Tapas

MAP P.34, POCKET MAP D12.
Pl. Sant Josep Oriol 9. Ⓜ Liceu.
Ⓦ tallerdetapas.com.

The fashionable "tapas workshop" sucks in tourists with its pretty location by the church of Santa

Bar del Pi

María del Pi. There's a year-round outdoor terrace, while the open kitchen turns out reliable, market-fresh dishes, with fish a speciality at dinner, from grilled langoustine to seared tuna. There are other branches around town (including one at C/Argenteria 51 in the Born), though this was the first. €

Venus Delicatessen

MAP P.34, POCKET MAP D13.
C/d'Avinyó 25. ⓦ Liceu. ⓦ facebook.com/
VenusDelicatessenBarcelona.
Not a deli, despite the name, but it's a handy place serving Mediterranean bistro cuisine throughout the day and night. It's good for vegetarians – dishes like lasagne, couscous, moussaka and salads are mostly meat-free. €

Bars

L'Ascensor

MAP P.34, POCKET MAP E13.
C/Bellafila 3. ⓦ Jaume I.
ⓦ instagram.com/lascensorcoctelbar.
Sliding antique wooden elevator doors signal the entrance to "The Lift", but it's no theme bar – just an easy-going local hangout, great for a late-night drink.

Collage

MAP P.34, POCKET MAP E14.
C/Consellers 4. ⓦ Jaume I.
ⓦ collagecocktailbar.com.
A stylish vintage place with a relaxed, pleasant atmosphere. The knowledgeable bartenders will mix you a creative drink and offer insightful advice on mixing. If that piques your interest, you can even go to their cocktail-making class for a well-spent afternoon.

Milk

MAP P.34, POCKET MAP E14.
C/d'en Gignàs 21. ⓦ Jaume I.
ⓦ milkbarcelona.com.
Irish-owned bar and bistro that's carved a real niche as a welcoming neighbourhood hangout. Decor, they say, is that of a "millionaire's drawing room", with its sofas, cushions and antique chandeliers. Get there early for the famously relaxed brunch, or there's dinner and cocktails every night to a funky soundtrack.

Harlem Jazz Club

Pipa Club

MAP P.34, POCKET MAP C13.
Pl. Reial 3. Ⓜ Liceu. Ⓦ pipaclub.es.
Historically a pipe-smoker's haunt, it's a wood-panelled, slick kind of place for late-night cocktails – ring the bell to be let in and make your way up the stairs.

Zim

MAP P.34, POCKET MAP E13.
C/Daguería 20. Ⓜ Jaume I.
A tiny, hole-in-the-wall tasting bar for selected wines from boutique producers. It can be a real squeeze, and hours are somewhat flexible, but for a reviving glass or two accompanied by farmhouse cheese, cured meat and artisan-made bread, you can't beat it.

Clubs

Harlem Jazz Club

MAP P.34, POCKET MAP D13.
C/Comtessa de Sobradiel 8. Ⓜ Jaume I.
Ⓦ harlemjazzclub.es.
For many years *the* hot place for jazz, where every style gets an airing, from African and Gypsy to flamenco and fusion. Live music Tues–Sun at 10.30pm and midnight (weekends 11.30pm & 2am). Entry charge depends on the night and the act.

Jamboree

MAP P.34, POCKET MAP C13.
Pl. Reial 17. Ⓜ Liceu. Ⓦ masimas.com.
They don't get the big jazz names here that they used to, but the nightly gigs (at 8pm & 10pm) still pull in the crowds, while the wild Monday-night WTF jazz, funk and hip-hop jam session (from 8pm) is a city fixture. Stay on for the club, which kicks in after midnight and you get funky sounds and retro pop, rock and disco until 5am. Entry charge varies.

La Macarena

MAP P.34, POCKET MAP D14.
C/Nou de Sant Francesc 5. Ⓜ Drassanes.

Tarantos

Ⓦ macarenaclub.com.
Once a place where flamenco tunes were offered up to La Macarena, the Virgin of Seville – now, a tiny, heaving temple to all things electro. Entry free until around 1am.

Sidecar

MAP P.34, POCKET MAP D13.
Pl. Reial 7. Ⓜ Liceu. Ⓦ sidecar.es.
Hip music club – pronounced "See-day-car" – with gigs (usually at 10.30pm) and DJs (from 12.30am) that champion rock, indie, roots and fusion acts, so a good place to check out the latest Catalan hip-hop, rumba and flamenco sounds. Entry charge varies.

Tarantos

MAP P.34, POCKET MAP C13.
Pl. Reial 17. Ⓜ Liceu. Ⓦ masimas.com.
Jamboree's sister club is the place for short, exuberant flamenco tasters, where young singers, dancers and guitarists perform nightly at 8.30pm, 9.30pm & 10.30pm (with extra sessions in July and August). Purists are a bit sniffy, but it's a great introduction to the scene. Entry charge.

Port Vell and Barceloneta

Barcelona has an urban waterfront that merges seamlessly with the Old Town, providing an easy escape from the claustrophobic medieval streets. The harbour at the bottom of La Rambla has been thoroughly overhauled in recent years and Port Vell (Old Port), as it's now known, presents a series of heavyweight tourist attractions, from sightseeing boats and maritime museum to the aquarium. By way of contrast, Barceloneta – the wedge of land to the east, backing the marina – retains its eighteenth-century character, and the former fishing quarter is still the most popular place to come and eat paella, fish and seafood. Metro Drassanes, at the bottom of La Rambla, is the best starting point for Port Vell; Barceloneta has its own metro station.

Mirador de Colom

MAP P.48, POCKET MAP C15.
Pl. Portal de la Pau. Ⓜ Drassanes.
Ⓦ bit.ly/MiradorColom. Charge.

The monument at the foot of La Rambla commemorates the visit made by Christopher Columbus in June 1493, when the navigator received a royal welcome in Barcelona. Columbus

Mirador de Colom

tops a grandiose iron column, 52m high, guarded by lions, and you can ride the lift up to the panoramic viewing platform at Columbus's feet. Meanwhile, from the quayside in front of the Columbus monument, Las Golondrinas sightseeing boats depart on regular trips throughout the year around the inner harbour.

Museu Marítim

MAP P.48, POCKET MAP B14/15.
Av. de les Drassanes. Ⓜ Drassanes.
Ⓦ mmb.cat. Charge, free Sun after 3pm.

Barcelona's medieval shipyards, or *drassanes*, were in continuous use – fitting and arming Catalunya's war fleet or trading vessels – until well into the eighteenth century. Once waterside, they now lie 100m back from the Mediterranean thanks to the city's ever-expanding concrete sprawl. The stone-vaulted buildings make a fitting, and handsome, home for the excellent Maritime Museum. There's a regularly changing schedule of temporary exhibitions, plus a range of activities, such as navigation and stargazing, that can be booked through the website. The museum entry ticket also includes a short

Museu Marítim

tour of the *Santa Eulàlia*, a vintage three-masted schooner moored down on the Moll de la Fusta harbourside (check hours at the museum). The courtyard café is a particularly pleasant spot to pass a quiet hour or two.

L'Aquàrium

MAP P.48, POCKET MAP G8–H8.
Moll d'Espanya. Ⓜ Drassanes.
Ⓦ aquariumbcn.com. Charge.
Port Vell's high-profile aquarium drags in families and school parties throughout the year to see "a magical world, full of mystery". Or, to be more precise, to see 11,000 fish and sea creatures in 35 themed tanks representing underwater caves, tropical reefs and other maritime habitats. It's vastly overpriced, and despite the claims of excellence, it offers few new experiences, save perhaps the 80-metre-long walk-through underwater tunnel, which brings you face to face with gliding rays and cruising sharks.

Maremàgnum

MAP P.48, POCKET MAP G8.
Moll d'Espanya. Ⓜ Drassanes.
Ⓦ maremagnum.es. Free.
From near the Columbus statue, the wooden Rambla de Mar swing bridge strides across the harbour to the Maremàgnum mall and leisure centre on Moll d'Espanya. It's a typically bold piece of Catalan design, its soaring glass lines tempered by the undulating wooden walkways that provide scintillating views back across the harbour to the city. Inside there are two floors of gift shops and boutiques, plus a range of cafés and fast-food outlets.

Stroll further along the Moll d'Espanya and you'll find a huge wooden scale model of *Ictineo II*, the world's first real functioning submarine. It was built in 1862 by luckless local inventor Narcis Monturiol I Estarriol, whose company went bankrupt before he could benefit from his work of engineering genius.

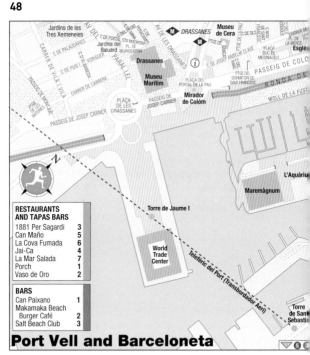

RESTAURANTS
AND TAPAS BARS
1881 Per Sagardi	3
Can Maño	5
La Cova Fumada	6
Jai-Ca	4
La Mar Salada	7
Porch	1
Vaso de Oro	2

BARS
Can Paixano	1
Makamaka Beach Burger Café	2
Salt Beach Club	3

Port Vell and Barceloneta

Museu d'Història de Catalunya

MAP P.48, POCKET MAP F15.
Palau de Mar, Pl. de Pau Vila 3.
Ⓜ Barceloneta. Ⓦ mhcat.net. Charge, free for under-16s and on first Sun of month 10am–2.30pm.

A dramatic harbourside warehouse conversion contains a museum tracing the history of Catalunya from the Stone Age to the present day. Poke around the interior of a Roman grain ship or compare the rival nineteenth-century architectural plans for the Eixample. The *1881 Per Sagardi*

Basque restaurant on the top floor – no museum ticket needed – boasts glorious views over the port from its terrace, a top spot for sunset cocktails.

Barceloneta

MAP P.48, POCKET MAP H8–J7.
Ⓜ Barceloneta.

There's no finer place for lunch on a sunny day than Barceloneta, an eighteenth-century neighbourhood of tightly packed, gridded streets with bustling harbour on one side and sandy beach on the other. There's a local market, the **Mercat**

The cross-harbour cable car

The most thrilling ride in the city is across the harbour on the Telefèric del Port (Transbordador Aeri), or cable car, which sweeps from the Sant Sebastià tower at the foot of Barceloneta to Montjuïc. Departures are every 15min (Ⓦ telefericodebarcelona. com; charge), but expect queues in summer and at weekends as the cars only carry about twenty people at a time.

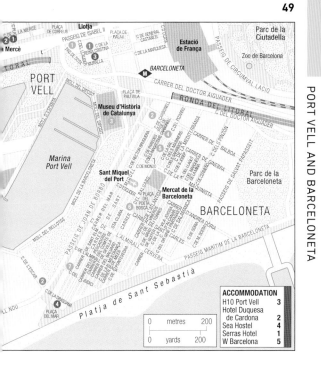

ACCOMMODATION

H10 Port Vell	3
Hotel Duquesa de Cardona	2
Sea Hostel	4
Serras Hotel	1
W Barcelona	5

de la Barceloneta (Mon–Sat), with a couple of excellent bars and restaurants, while Barceloneta's famous seafood restaurants are found across the neighbourhood, but most characteristically lined along the harbourside Passeig Joan de Borbó.

Platja de Sant Sebastià

MAP P.48, POCKET MAP G9–K8.
Ⓜ Barceloneta.

Barceloneta's beach – the first in a series of sandy city beaches – curves from the flanks of the neighbourhood, past the swimming pools of the Club Natació and out to the landmark sail-shaped *W Barcelona* hotel. Closer to the Barceloneta end there are beach bars, outdoor cafés and sculptures, while a double row of palms backs the esplanade that runs above the sands as far as the Port Olímpic (a 15min walk). Bladers, skaters, joggers and cyclists have one of the Med's best views for company.

Cross-harbour cable car

Restaurants and tapas bars

1881 Per Sagardi

MAP P.48, POCKET MAP F15.
Pl. de Pau Vila 3. Ⓜ Barceloneta.
Ⓦ gruposagardi.com.
Head to the roof of the waterfront Museu d'Història de Catalunya and you'll be met with the smell of wood smoke at this grill-led restaurant. It's worth paying for a pricey meal here just to sit on the terrace with a Martini and watch the yachts sailing in and out of the harbour. €€€

Can Maño

MAP P.48, POCKET MAP F15.
C/Baluard 12. Ⓜ Barceloneta.
Ⓦ instagram.com/can_mano.
There's rarely a tourist in sight in this classic old-fashioned diner. It's an authentic, no-frills experience with a choice of fried or grilled fish, supplemented by a few daily seafood specials and basic meat dishes. €€

Paella negra

La Cova Fumada

MAP P.48, POCKET MAP H8.
C/Baluard 56. Ⓜ Barceloneta.
Ⓦ lacovafumada.com.
Behind brown wooden doors on the market square (there's no sign) is this rough-and-ready tavern with battered marble tables and antique barrels. That it's always packed is a testament to the quality of the market-fresh tapas, from the griddled prawns to the *bomba* (spicy potato meatball). Arrive early for any chance of a table. €

Jai-Ca

MAP P.48, POCKET MAP F15.
C/Ginebra 9 & 13. Ⓜ Barceloneta.
Ⓦ barjaica.com.
A great choice for tapas, with bundles of razor clams, stuffed mussels, crisp baby squid and other seafood platters. €

La Mar Salada

MAP P.48, POCKET MAP H8.
Pg. de Joan de Borbó 58. Ⓜ Barceloneta.
Ⓦ lamarsalada.cat.
While many of the restaurants in Barceloneta have let standards slip, *La Mar Salada* has instead raised the bar. Buying freshly landed fish straight from the dock directly opposite, the chefs offer creative seafood dishes at bargain prices. The lunchtime set menu is superb value, and there's even a sunny terrace to eat it on. €€€

Porch

MAP P.48, POCKET MAP E14.
Pas de Sota Muralla 1. Ⓜ Barceloneta.
Ⓦ instagram.com/porchbcn.
A cocktail and tapas bar catering to a young and predominantly foreign crowd, who fill its leafy terrace on the way back from the beach. A short list of tapas, salads and *pinsas* (small pizzas) provide a good excuse to linger awhile. €€

Vaso de Oro

MAP P.48, POCKET MAP F15.
C/Balboa 6. Ⓜ Barceloneta.
Ⓦ instagram.com/elvasodeoro.barcelona.

An old favourite for stand-up tapas – there's no menu, but order the *patatas bravas*, some thick slices of fried sausage, grilled shellfish and a dollop of tuna salad and you've touched all the bases. Unusually, you'll find that they also brew their own beer; light and dark. €

Bars

Can Paixano

MAP P.48, POCKET MAP E14.
C/de la Reina Cristina 7. Ⓜ Barceloneta.
Ⓦ canpaixano.com.

A must on everyone's itinerary is this counter-only joint where the drink of choice – all right, the only drink – is cava by the glass or bottle. It's popular, so you may have to fight your way in, but this congenial, lively place is a family business that's been producing their own cheap and cheerful cava for more than 50 years. Drinkers must also order something from the long list of excellent, hot sandwiches – bacon, cheese, sausage and so on.

Makamaka Beach Burger Café

MAP P.48, POCKET MAP H8.
Pg. de Joan de Borbó 76. Ⓜ Barceloneta.
Ⓦ makamaka.es.

You really can't ask for more: creative cocktails and some of the city's finest burgers served on a

Can Paixano

large, beachside *terrassa*. Laidback, late night and lots of fun; it's Hawaii-meets-Barcelona.

Salt Beach Club

MAP P.48, POCKET MAP G9.
Pg. del Mare Nostrum 19–21.
Ⓜ Barceloneta. Ⓦ saltbeachclub.com.

More famous for their – slightly pricey – drinks than their food, this beachfront bar with a beautiful ocean view and seats right in the sand makes for a pleasant place to have a drink on a cloudless evening.

It takes two

You want a seafood paella or an *arròs negre* (black rice with squid ink), or maybe a garlicky *fideuà* (noodles with seafood) – of course you do. Problem is, you're on your own and virtually every restaurant that offers these classic Barcelona dishes does so for a minimum of two people (often you don't find out until you examine the menu's small print). Solution? Ask the waiter upfront, as sometimes the kitchen will oblige single diners, or look for the dishes on a *menú del dia* (especially on Thurs, traditionally rice day), when there should be no minimum. Probably best not to grab a stranger off the street to share a paella, however desperate you are.

El Raval

The Old Town area west of La Rambla is known as El Raval (from the Arabic word for suburb), and has always formed a world apart from the nobler Gothic quarter. Traditionally a red-light area, and once notorious for its sleazy Barri Xinès (China Town), it still has some very seedy corners (particularly south of Carrer de Sant Pau), though it's changing rapidly, notably in the "upper Raval" around Barcelona's contemporary art museum, the MACBA. Cutting-edge galleries, designer restaurants and fashionable bars are all part of the scene these days, while an arty, affluent crowd rubs shoulders with the area's Asian and North African immigrants and the older, traditional residents. Metro stations Catalunya, Liceu, Drassanes and Paral·lel serve the neighbourhood.

Museu d'Art Contemporani de Barcelona (MACBA)

MAP P.54, POCKET MAP B10/11–C10/11.
Pl. dels Àngels 1. Ⓜ Catalunya.
Ⓦ macba.cat. Charge.

This iconic contemporary art museum – with a stark main facade constructed entirely of glass – anchors the regenerated upper Raval. The collection represents the main movements in art since 1945, mainly (but not exclusively) in Catalunya and Spain, and depending on the changing exhibitions you may catch works by major names such as Joan Miró, Antoni Tàpies or Eduardo Chillida. Joan Brossa, leading light

Museu d'Art Contemporani de Barcelona

of the Catalan Dau al Set group of the 1950s, also has work here. There are free guided tours of the permanent collection (tour times vary; check website for details), and a good museum shop.

Filmoteca de Catalunya

MAP P.54, POCKET MAP B13.
Pl. Salvador Seguí 1–9. Ⓜ Liceu.
Ⓦ filmoteca.cat. Charge.

The Josep Lluís Mateo-designed Filmoteca de Catalunya marks yet another step in the government's push to revitalize El Raval. Opened in 2012, the building has two below-ground cinemas, as well as a film library, a bookshop and spaces for permanent and temporary cinema-related exhibitions. All the films – a mix of vintage classics and slightly more contemporary arthouse films – are shown in their original language with Spanish or Catalan subtitles.

Centre de Cultura Contemporània de Barcelona (CCCB)

MAP P.54, POCKET MAP B10–C10.
C/Montalegre 5. Ⓜ Catalunya. Ⓦ cccb.org.
Charge, free Sun after 3pm.

There's a wide range of city-related exhibitions on show at the contemporary culture centre (ranging from photography to architecture), as well as a varied cinema, concert and festival programme. The imaginatively restored building was once an infamous workhouse and asylum, and the main courtyard still retains its old tile panels and presiding statue of

Exhibit at the CCCB

patron saint, Sant Jordi. At the back, the *Terracccita* café-bar makes the most of its terrace overlooking the modern square joining the CCCB to MACBA.

Plaça de Vicenç Martorell

MAP P.54, POCKET MAP C11.
Ⓜ Catalunya.

El Raval's nicest traffic-free square lies just a few minutes' walk from the MACBA. The small playground here is well used by local families, and the arcaded square features a first-rate café, the *Kasparo* – a real find if you're looking for a break from sightseeing. Meanwhile, around the corner are several other cafés, while the narrow **Carrer del Bonsuccés**, **Carrer Sitges** and **Carrer dels Tallers** house a

The beat from the street

The Barcelona sound – *mestiza* – is a cross-cultural musical fusion whose heartland is the immigrant melting-pot of El Raval. Parisian-born Barcelona resident Manu Chao kickstarted the whole genre, but check out the Carrer dels Tallers music stores for the other flag-bearers – Cheb Balowski (Algerian–Catalan fusion), Ojos de Brujo (Catalan flamenco and rumba), GoLem System (dub/reggae) and Macaco (rumba, raga, hip-hop).

EL RAVAL

El Raval

CARRER DE FLORIDABLANCA

C CASANOVA

C DE VALLDONZE

C DE VILLARROEL

SANT ANTONI

CARRER DEL LLEÓ

La Paloma
Sala de Ball

PTGE DE
SANT ANTONI ABAT

RONDA DE

PLAÇA DEL
PES DE
LA PALLA

CARRER DE LA PALM

SANT ANTONI

CARRER DEL COMTE D'URGELL

C DE TAMARIT

C DE SANT ERASME

C DE SANT VICENÇ

CARRER DE FERLANDIN

C NOU DE DULCE

PLAÇA
DEL DUBTE

CARRER DE SANT GIL

C CARDONA

CARRER DE LA LLUNA

C DE GU

Mercat de
Sant Antoni

PLAÇA
DEL DUBTE

SANT ANTONI

C DEL PRINCEP

C REQUESENS

CARRER DE LA CENDRA

DE VIAN4

CARRER DE LA RIERA ALTA

CARRER

CARRER DE LA BISBE LAGUARDA

C D'ERASME DE JANER

CARRER DE SANT ANTONI ABAT

CARRER DELS SALVADOR

C DE SANT CLIMENT

C D'EN BOTELLA

PLAÇA DEL
PEDRO

DE SANT
LLÀTZER

CARRER DEL CARM

CARRER DE LA CERA

CARRER DE L'HOSPITAL

CARRER DE VISTALEGRE

CARRER DE

L'AURORA

CARRER DE LA REINA AMALIA

CARRER DE LES CARRETES

C DE SANT PACIÀ

CARRER DE
LA RIERETA

CARRER DE
SANT RAFAEL

C DE SANT MARTI

C DE
SANT BARTOMEU

RAMBLA DEL RAVAL

RONDA DE SANT PAU

C DE LA LLEIALTAT

PLAÇA DE
JOSEP MARIA
FOLCH I TORRES

PLAÇ
VÁZC
MONTA

C DE SANTA ELENA

CARRER DE LES FLORS

CARRER DE SANT PAU

CARR

AVINGUDA DEL PARAL.LEL

C D'EN FONTRODONA

CARRER DE VILA I VILÀ

CARRER DE L'ABAT SAFONT

Església de
Sant Pau
del Camp

C DE L'HORT D'EN PAU

CARRER DE SANT OLEGUER

C

PARAL.LEL

CARRER DE LES TÀPIES

PARAL.LEL

CARRER NOU DE LA RAMBLA

Funicular
de Montjuïc

C DE SANTA MADRONA

CARRER DEL LOM

| 0 | metres | 100 |
| 0 | yards | 100 |

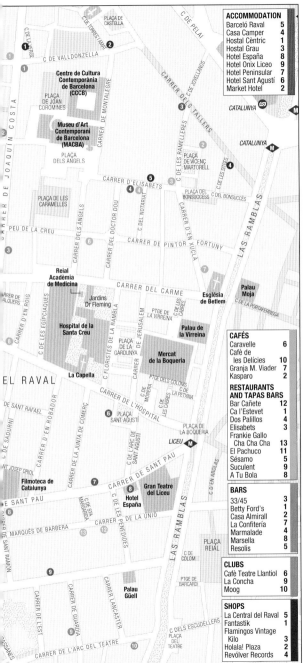

El Gato del Raval

concentrated selection of the city's best independent music stores, and urban- and street-wear shops.

Hospital de la Santa Creu

MAP P.54, POCKET MAP B12–C12.
Entrances on C/del Carme and C/de l'Hospital. Ⓜ Liceu. Free.
The neighbourhood's most historic relic is the Gothic hospital complex founded in 1402. After the hospital shifted location in 1930, the buildings were subsequently converted to cultural and educational use (including the Catalan national library), and visitors and students now wander freely through the charming medieval cloistered garden. Inside the Carrer del Carme entrance (on the right) you can see some superb seventeenth-century decorative tiles, while opposite is a remarkable eighteenth-century anatomical theatre inside the **Reial Acadèmia de Medicina** (open Wed and Sat morning only, free, ring the bell). The hospital's former chapel, **La Capella** (entered separately from Carrer de l'Hospital), is an exhibition space for new contemporary artists.

Rambla del Raval

MAP P.54, POCKET MAP B12–13.
Ⓜ Liceu.
The most obvious manifestation of the changing character of El Raval is the palm-lined boulevard that was gouged through former tenements and alleys, providing a huge pedestrianized space between Carrer de l'Hospital and Carrer de Sant Pau. The *rambla* has a distinct character all of its own, mixing kebab joints, phone shops and grocery stores with an increasing number of fashionable cafés and bars. Its signature building, halfway down, is the glow-in-the-dark, designer *Barceló Raval* hotel, while kids find it hard to resist a clamber on the bulbous cat sculpture. A weekend street market (selling everything from samosas to hammocks) adds a bit more character.

Just off the top of the *rambla*, **Carrer de la Riera Baixa** is at the centre of the city's second-hand/ vintage clothing scene. A dozen funky little independent clothes

High-society hotel

Some of the most influential names in Catalan *modernista* design came together to transform the dowdy nineteenth-century **Hotel España** (map p.54, pocket map C13; C/de Sant Pau 9–11; Ⓦ hotelespanya.com) into one of the city's most lavish addresses. With a gloriously tiled dining room, an amazing marble fireplace and a mural-clad ballroom, the hotel was the fashionable sensation of its day. A contemporary restoration has done a wonderful job of showing off the classy interior – try lunch in the hotel restaurant or a drink in the bar for a sneak peek.

shops provide the scope for an hour's browsing.

Palau Güell

MAP P.54, POCKET MAP C13.
C/Nou de la Rambla 3–5. Ⓜ Liceu.
Ⓦ palauguell.cat. Charge, free first Sun of the month.

El Raval's outstanding building is the extraordinary townhouse designed (1886–90) by the young Antoni Gaudí for a wealthy industrialist. At a time when other architects sought to conceal the iron supports within buildings, Gaudí displayed them instead as decorative features. Columns, arches and ceilings are all shaped and twisted in an elaborate style that was to become the hallmark of Gaudí's later works, while the roof terrace culminates in a fantastical series of tiled chimneys. Visitor numbers are limited – expect to queue or to receive a time-specific ticket.

Església de Sant Pau del Camp

MAP P.54, POCKET MAP A13.
C/de Sant Pau 101. Ⓜ Paral.lel.
☎ 934 410 001. Charge.

The unusual name of the church of Sant Pau del Camp (St Paul of the Field) is a graphic reminder that it once stood in open countryside beyond the city walls. Sant Pau was a Benedictine foundation of the tenth century, and above the main entrance are primitive thirteenth-century carvings of fish, birds and faces, while others adorn the charming cloister.

Mercat de Sant Antoni

MAP P.54, POCKET MAP E5.
C/del Comte d'Urgell 1. Ⓜ Sant Antoni.
Ⓦ mercatdesantantoni.com.

The neighbourhood's impressive nineteenth-century produce market is another that's been entirely remodelled and reopened. The new central foyer is designed to accentuate the remaining nineteenth-century structure. There are stalls with fresh produce and a flea market, and on Sundays, a book market outside the building. The traditional bolt hole is *Els Tres Tombs*, the restaurant-bar on the corner of Ronda de Sant Antoni, frequented by a good-natured mix of locals, market traders and tourists.

Palau Güell

Shops

La Central del Raval

MAP P.54, POCKET MAP C11.
C/d'Elisabets 6. Ⓜ Catalunya.
Ⓦ lacentral.com.
Occupying a unique space in the former Misericòrdia chapel, this is a fantastically stocked arts and humanities treasure trove, with books piled high in every nook and cranny and a big English-language section. There are further outlets in MACBA (art museum) and MUHBA (history museum). The semi-secret café-bar out back is a great place to flick through a new purchase.

Fantastik

MAP P.54, POCKET MAP B10.
C/Joaquin Costa 62. Ⓜ Universitat.
Ⓦ fantastik.es.
Beguiling gifts, crafts and covetable objects from four continents. You'll never know how you lived without them, whether it's Chinese robots, African baskets, Russian domino sets or Vietnamese kitchen scales.

Granja M. Viader

Flamingos Vintage Kilo

MAP P.54, POCKET MAP B11.
C/dels Tallers 31. Ⓜ Catalunya.
Ⓦ vintagekilo.com.
Trendy second-hand vintage clothing from the 70s and 80s sold by the kilo, ranging from biker jackets to Hawaiian shirts. The stock is varied, stylish and carefully selected with a lot of North American gems.

Holala! Plaza

MAP P.54, POCKET MAP C10.
Pl. Castella 2. Ⓜ Universitat. Ⓦ holala-ibiza.com.
Vintage heaven in a warehouse setting (up past CCCB), for denim, flying jackets, Hawaiian shirts, baseball gear and much, much more. Also check out the other Raval store at Carrer dels Tallers 73.

Revólver Records

MAP P.54, POCKET MAP C11.
C/dels Tallers 11. Ⓜ Catalunya.
Ⓦ revolverrecords.es.
Revólver Records sells the city's best selection of vinyl and CDs at the lowest prices. It's defiantly old school: a record shop like they used to make them.

Cafés

Caravelle

MAP P.54, POCKET MAP B13.
C/Pintor Fortuny 31. Ⓜ Catalunya.
Ⓦ caravellebcn.com.
A place with a slightly hipster vibe, sparse but elegant decor and shared tables. Offers delicious, varied brunches and lunch dishes from lamb shawarma to chicken schnitzel, and also brews its own beer. €

Cafè de les Delícies

MAP P.54, POCKET MAP B13.
Rambla de Raval 47. Ⓜ Liceu. ☎ 934 415 714.
One of the first off the blocks in this revamped neighbourhood,

and still perhaps the best, plonking thrift-shop chairs and tables beneath exposed pipes and girders and coming up with something cute, cosy, mellow and arty. Locals meet for breakfast, sandwiches and tapas. €

Granja M. Viader

MAP P.54, POCKET MAP C11.
C/Xuclà 4–6. ⓜ Catalunya.
ⓦ granjaviader.cat.

The oldest traditional *granja* (milk bar) in town is a real historical survivor – it has a plaque outside for services to the city. The original owner was the inventor of "Cacaolat" (bottled chocolate milk), but you could also try *mel i mató* (curd cheese and honey). €

Kasparo

MAP P.54, POCKET MAP C11.
Pl. Vicenç Martorell 4. ⓜ Catalunya.
ⓦ acebook.com/kasparobcn.

A place to relax, in the arcaded corner of a quiet square, with outdoor seating year-round. There's muesli, Greek yoghurt and toast and jam for early birds. Later, sandwiches, tapas and assorted *platos del dia* (dishes of the day) are on offer – things like hummus and bread, vegetable quiche or couscous. €

Restaurants and tapas bars

Bar Cañete

MAP P.54, POCKET MAP C13.
C/de la Unió 17. ⓜ Liceu.
ⓦ barcanete.com.

Gleaming mirrors, dark wood furnishings and white-clad waiters set the scene for some of the city's classiest tapas, featuring premium ingredients (and pricetags to match, if you don't choose carefully). Take your pick from classic seafood and meat dishes sourced fresh from the local market. €€€

Bar Cañete

Ca l'Estevet

MAP P.54, POCKET MAP B10.
C/Valldonzella 46. ⓜ Universitat.
ⓦ restaurantestevet.com.

Ca l'Estevet, an unshifting rock in the fickle seas of foodie fashions, has been serving up old-school Catalan cuisine since 1940 (and, under a different name, for 50 years before that). The practice has made perfect; try the lunch menu or tuck into grilled *botifarra* sausages, roasted kid or *escudella i carn d'olla* (meat stew). €€€

Dos Palillos

MAP P.54, POCKET MAP C11.
C/d'Elisabets 9. ⓜ Catalunya.
ⓦ dospalillos.com.

Albert Raurich, former *chef de cuisine* at "world's best restaurant" *El Bulli*, swapped Catalan food for Asian fusion after falling in love with Japan. Try his à la carte dim sum in the front galley bar (from steamed dumplings to grilled oysters and various nigiri sushi)

Betty Ford's bar

or book for the back room where tasting menus wade their way through the highlights. €€€€

Elisabets

MAP P.54, POCKET MAP C11.
C/d'Elisabets 2. Ⓜ Catalunya.
Ⓦ elisabets1962.com.
Reliable Catalan home cooking served at cramped tables in a jovial dining room. Everyone piles in early for breakfast, the hearty lunch is hard to beat for price, or you can just have tapas, sandwiches and drinks at the bar. €€

Frankie Gallo Cha Cha Cha

MAP P.54, POCKET MAP C11.
C/Marquès de Barberà 15. Ⓜ Liceu.
Ⓦ frankiegallochachacha.com.
A long-time, jumping pizza joint with a disco aesthetic but a very serious attitude to their artisanal pizzas, which they describe as "transgressive pineapple-free creations". Prices are reasonable, portions large and the approach eco-friendly. €€

El Pachuco

MAP P.54, POCKET MAP A13.
C/de Sant Pau 110. Ⓜ Liceu.
Ⓦ elpachuco.bar.

A tiny place with authentic Mexican cuisine. Great tacos and amazing quesadillas attract crowds, so be ready for a long (up to 1.5hrs) wait at its most crowded – but be patient, it's definitely worth it. The experience will be complete if you order a margarita cocktail, too. Cash only. €

Sésamo

MAP P.54, POCKET MAP A11.
C/Sant Antoni Abat 52. Ⓜ Sant Antoni.
Ⓦ bit.ly/SesamoBarcelona.
A classy fusion tapas place offering up a vegetarian-orientated chalkboard menu of innovative dishes that roll out of an open kitchen. Try vegetable-stuffed courgette rolls (a sort of Catalan sushi), slow-roast tomato tart or daily risotto and pasta dishes. The Catalan wines and cheeses are a high point too. €€

Suculent

MAP P.54, POCKET MAP B13.
Rambla de Raval 43. Ⓜ Liceu.
Ⓦ suculent.com.
As well as meaning "succulent", the name of this bistro is a play on the Catalan words *sucar lent* – to dip slowly – and you'll do just that, using fresh, warm bread to mop up sauces from dish after lip-smacking dish. The steak tartare on grilled marrowbone will put hairs on your chest and bring tears of joy to your eyes. €€€

A Tu Bola

MAP P.54, POCKET MAP B12.
C/de Hospital 78. Ⓜ Liceu.
Ⓦ atubolarest.com.
Falafel-like balls of fresh ingredients come in unexpected but delightful flavour combinations here, while home-made harissa and soft drinks bear hallmarks of the attention to detail that lifts this far above typical street-food standard. There aren't many seats and prices are low, so expect a wait at busy times. €

Bars

33/45

MAP P.54, POCKET MAP C11.
C/Joaquín Costa 4. Ⓜ Catalunya.
Ⓦ 3345.es.

Part bar, part gallery, the *33/45* is something of an El Raval institution, and a favoured meeting spot for lazy Sunday mornings. As the name suggests, the bar is of a musical bent, with DJs, pop-up record stores and occasional live music.

Betty Ford's

MAP P.54, POCKET MAP B10.
C/de Joaquín Costa 56. Ⓜ Universitat.
Ⓦ bettyfordsbcn.com.

With a friendly, welcoming atmosphere and a vibe somewhere between a student lounge and a beach bar, *Betty Ford's* is full of bouncy young things sipping colourful cocktails and cold Australian beer. You can deal with the late-night munchies by getting to grips with their famed burger menu.

A Tu Bola

Casa Almirall

MAP P.54, POCKET MAP B11.
C/de Joaquin Costa 33. Ⓜ Universitat.
Ⓦ casaalmirall.com.

Dating from 1860, Barcelona's oldest bar is a *modernista* classic – make sure you check out the ornate doors, marble counter, vintage furniture and stupendous, glittering bar. It's long been a venerated leftist hangout and because it's not too young and not too loud, it's always good for a late-night drink away from the party crowd.

La Confitería

MAP P.54, POCKET MAP A13.
C/de Sant Pau 128. Ⓜ Paral·lel.
Ⓦ confiteria.cat.

This former bakery and confectioner's – carved wood bar, faded tile floor, murals, antique chandeliers and mirrored cabinets – is now a popular bar and meeting point. It's out on a limb in El Raval, but the glorious interior is certainly worth a detour, and it's a handy stop-off in any case on the way to a night out in Poble Sec.

EL RAVAL

Marmalade

MAP P.54, POCKET MAP B11.
C/de Riera Alta 4–6. Ⓜ Sant Antoni.
Ⓦ marmaladebarcelona.com.

A hugely glam facelift for the old Muebles Navarro furniture store goes for big, church-like spaces and a backlit Art Deco bar that resembles a high altar. Cocktails, bistro meals and gourmet burgers pull in a relaxed dine-and-lounge crowd, and there's a popular weekend brunch too. If you like the style, give the more informal Barri Gòtic sister bar, *Milk*, a whirl.

Marsella

MAP P.54, POCKET MAP B13.
C/de Sant Pau 65. Ⓜ Liceu.
Ⓦ instagram.com/barmarsella.

Authentic, atmospheric, sleaze-period bar – named after the French port of Marseilles – where absinthe is the drink of choice. It's frequented by a spirited mix of oddball locals and young trendies, all looking for a slice of the old Barri Xinès.

Resolis

MAP P.54, POCKET MAP B11.
C/Riera Baixa 22. Ⓜ Sant Antoni.
Ⓦ resolisbar.com.

A decayed, century-old bar turned into a cool hangout with decent

La Confitería

tapas, from veggie *bruschette* to steamed mussels. They didn't do much – a lick of paint, polish the panelling, patch up the brickwork – but now punters spill out of the door onto "secondhand clothes street" and a good time is had by all.

Clubs

Cafè Teatre Llantiol

MAP P.54, POCKET MAP A12.
C/de la Riereta 7. Ⓜ Sant Antoni.
Ⓦ llantiol.com.

Local-language theatre isn't accessible to non-speakers, but you might want to give this idiosyncratic café-cabaret a try. As well as Catalan-language plays, there are shows featuring a mix of mime, song, clowning, magic and dance, and sometimes there's English-language stand-up comedy too.

La Concha

MAP P.54, POCKET MAP B13.
C/de la Guardia 14. Ⓜ Drassanes.
Ⓦ laconchadelraval.com.

The Arab-flamenco fusion here creates a great atmosphere, worth braving the slightly dodgy area for. It's a kitsch, gay-friendly joint,

La Paloma

La Paloma Sala de Ball

La Paloma holds the distinction of being the oldest functioning ballroom and nightclub in Europe, with a history dating back to 1903.

The venue's interior exudes luxury, adorned with lavish furnishings reminiscent of the Hall of Mirrors at Versailles. It boasts intricate garlands, botanical motifs and frescoes depicting various styles of traditional Catalan dance. One of its most iconic features is the grand chandelier that gracefully suspends from the centre of the room.

Located at Carrer del Tigre, 27, La Paloma hosts a diverse array of events on a weekly basis, including traditional balls featuring a live orchestra, club nights with contemporary electronic music, and concerts catering to various tastes.

Visitors are encouraged to explore the venue, which offers multiple vantage points for enjoying the entertainment. You can take in the show from the first-floor viewing balcony, relax in the booths on the ground floor, or hit the dance floor, depending on your preferences.

Tickets from €13, depending on the session. For group bookings ☎ 933 01 68 97. For more information, visit ⓦ lapaloma.com or follow us on Instagram @lapalomabcn

dedicated to the "incandescent presence" of Sara Montiel, queen of song and cinema (and LGBTQ+ icon), with uninhibited dancing by tourists and locals alike. Free entry.

Moog
MAP P.54, POCKET MAP C14.

C/Arc del Teatre 3. ⓂDrassanes. ⓦmasimas.com.
Small but influential club with a minimalist look, playing techno, electro, drum 'n' bass and trance to a cool but up-for-it crowd. There's a second, less manic dancefloor as well. Entry charge.

Sant Pere

Perhaps the least visited part of the Old Town is the medieval *barri* of Sant Pere, the area that lies immediately north of the Barri Gòtic and across Carrer de la Princesa from La Ribera. It has two remarkable buildings – the *modernista* concert hall, known as the Palau de la Música Catalana, and the stylishly designed neighbourhood market, Mercat Santa Caterina. There's been much regeneration in the *barri* over recent years, and it's well worth an afternoon's stroll or a night out, with new boulevards and community projects alongside DJ bars and designer shops. To walk through the neighbourhood, you can start at Metro Urquinaona, close to the Palau de la Música Catalana, with Metro Jaume I marking the southern end of Sant Pere.

Palau de la Música Catalana

MAP P.65, POCKET MAP E11.
C/Sant Pere Més Alt. Ⓜ Urquinaona.
Ⓦ palaumusica.org. Charge.

Barcelona's most extraordinary concert hall was built in 1908, to a design by visionary *modernista* architect Lluís Domènech i Montaner. The elaborate exterior is simply smothered in tiles and mosaics, while a mighty bulbous stained-glass skylight caps the second-storey auditorium (which contemporary critics claimed to be an engineering impossibility). The more modern Petit Palau offers a smaller auditorium space, while to the side a contemporary glass facade and courtyard provide the main public access. Concerts here (throughout the year) include

Palau de la Música Catalana

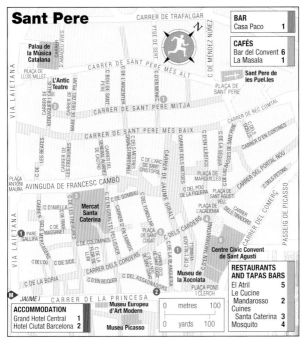

Sant Pere

BAR	
Casa Paco	1

CAFÉS	
Bar del Convent	6
La Masala	1

RESTAURANTS AND TAPAS BARS	
El Atril	5
Le Cucine Mandarosso	2
Cuines Santa Caterina	3
Mosquito	4

ACCOMMODATION	
Grand Hotel Central	1
Hotel Ciutat Barcelona	2

performances by the Orfeo Català choral group and the Barcelona city orchestra, though you can also catch anything from flamenco to world music. Numbers are limited on the very popular fifty-minute guided tours, so it's best to buy a ticket a day or two in advance (by phone, online or at the box office).

L'Antic Teatre

MAP P.65, POCKET MAP E11.
C/Verdaguer i Callis 12. Ⓜ Urquinaona.
Ⓦ anticteatre.com.

An independent theatre with a wildly original programme, from video shows and offbeat cabaret to modern dance and left-field music. The best bit may just be the magical, light-strung garden-bar, a real insiders' place, a little scruffy, but open to all.

Plaça de Sant Pere

MAP P.65, POCKET MAP G11.
Ⓜ Arc de Triomf.

The neighbourhood extends around three parallel medieval streets, Carrers de Sant Pere Més Alt (upper), Mitja (middle) and Baix (lower), which contain the bulk of the finest buildings and shops – a mixture of boutiques, textile shops, groceries and old family businesses. The streets all converge on the original neighbourhood square, Plaça de Sant Pere, whose foursquare church flanks one side, overlooking a flamboyant iron drinking fountain. Originally built in the shape of a Greek cross, the church, **Sant Pere de les Puel.les**, dates back to 945 AD and was the city's first convent of Benedictine nuns. It occasionally hosts concerts.

Mercat Santa Caterina

MAP P.65, POCKET MAP F12.
Av. Francesc Cambò 16. Ⓜ Jaume I.
Ⓦ mercatsantacaterina.com.

Mercat Santa Caterina

An eye-catching renovation of the neighbourhood market retained its original walls but added slatted wooden doors and windows and a dramatic multicoloured wave roof. It's one of the best places in the city to shop for food, and its market restaurant and bar are definitely worth a visit in any case. During renovation work, the foundations of a medieval convent were discovered here and the excavations are visible in the **Espai Santa Caterina** (Mon–Sat, free) at the rear of the market.

Plaça de Sant Agusti Vell

MAP P.65, POCKET MAP G12.
Ⓜ Jaume I.

The pretty, tree-shaded Plaça de Sant Agusti Vell sits in the middle of an ambitious urban regeneration project, which has transformed previously crowded alleys. To the north, locals tend organic allotments in the middle of the landscaped Pou de la Figuera square, while south down **Carrer d'Allada Vermell** are overarching trees, a children's playground and a series of outdoor cafés and bars. Meanwhile, running down from Plaça de Sant Agusti Vell, **Carrer dels Carders** – once "ropemakers' street" – is now a funky retail quarter mixing grocery stores, cafés, boutiques and craft shops.

Centre Cívic Convent de Sant Agusti

MAP P.65, POCKET MAP F12–G12.
C/del Comerç 36. Ⓜ Jaume I.
Ⓦ conventagusti.com. Admission charges vary, free for some events.

Driving many of the neighbourhood improvements is the community centre installed inside the revamped Convent de Sant Agusti, whose thirteenth-century cloister provides a unique performance space. There's a full cultural programme here, from workshops to concerts, with a particular emphasis on electronic and experimental music and art, and don't miss the excellent convent café.

Museu de la Xocolata

MAP P.65, POCKET MAP F12–G13.
C/del Comerç 36. Ⓜ Jaume I.
Ⓦ museuxocolata.cat. Charge.

Part of the Convent de Sant Agusti contains Barcelona's chocolate museum, which is a rather uninspiring plod through the history of the stuff. Whether you go in or not depends on how keen you are to see models of Gaudí buildings or religious icons sculpted in chocolate. There are some very nice chocs to buy in the shop though (free to enter), while at the adjacent Escola de Pastisseria, glass windows look onto the students learning their craft in the kitchens.

Cafés

Bar del Convent

MAP P.65, POCKET MAP G12.
Pl. de l'Acadèmia, C/del Comerç 36.
Ⓜ Jaume I. ☎ 932 565 017.
The cloister café-bar is a bargain for
lunch and light meals, with soups,
stir-fries, lasagne and couscous,
served indoors or on a child-friendly
terrace. In its latest reincarnation, it
is run by an organization that helps
people into the workplace. €

La Masala

MAP P.65, POCKET MAP F11.
C/Mònec 6. Ⓜ Urquinaona.
Ⓦ instagram.com/la_masala_cafe.
Named after the masala chai tea
they serve, *La Masala* is hidden
down a narrow sidestreet and is
mostly beautifully quiet. The actual
speciality here is excellent coffee, and
there's a short, simple list of breakfast
dishes and home-made cakes. €

Restaurants and tapas bars

El Atril

MAP P.65, POCKET MAP F12.
C/dels Carders 23. Ⓜ Jaume I.
Ⓦ elatrilbarcelona.es.
The "Music Stand" is a cosy bar-
restaurant complete with summer
terrassa and a selection of salads and
mostly grilled meats, from octopus
to kangaroo. Outside busy lunch and
dinner times, it's possible to just have
a selection of tapas (*patatas bravas*,
Padrón peppers and so on). €€

Le Cucine Mandarosso

MAP P.65, POCKET MAP E11.
C/de Verdaguer i Callís 4. Ⓜ Urquinaona.
Ⓦ lecucinemandarosso.com.
This little piece of Napoli in
Barcelona imports the southern
Italian city's characteristics:
crowded, friendly, cheap, charming
and single-minded about delicious,
simple food. No reservations at
lunchtime turns getting a table into
a lottery, but the good-value set
menu makes it worth trying. €€

Cuines Santa Caterina

MAP P.65, POCKET MAP F12.
Mercat Santa Caterina, Av. Francesc
Cambó 16 Ⓜ Jaume I Ⓦ grupotragaluz.com.
A ravishing open-plan tapas bar
and market restaurant with tables
under soaring rafters. Food touches
all bases – pasta to sushi, Catalan
rice to Thai curry – with most
things pretty reasonably priced. €€

Mosquito

MAP P.65, POCKET MAP F12.
C/dels Carders 46. Ⓜ Jaume I.
Ⓦ mosquitotapas.com.
Asian tapas bar with paper lanterns,
artisan beers and an authentic,
made-to-order dim sum menu,
from shrimp dumplings to tofu
rolls. The *pho* (only served at lunch
time) is highly recommended. €

Bar

Casa Paco

MAP P.65, POCKET MAP F12.
C/d'Allada Vermell 10. Ⓜ Jaume I.
☎ 933 149 320.
This little music joint is a hit on the
weekend DJ scene, though by day
its terrace is the favoured meeting
spot for the neighbourhood parents,
thanks to the adjacent playground.

Casa Paco

La Ribera

The traditional highlights of the old artisans' quarter of La Ribera are the Museu Picasso (one of Barcelona's biggest tourist attractions) and the graceful church of Basílica de Santa María del Mar. The cramped streets between the two were at the heart of medieval industry and commerce, and it's still the neighbourhood of choice for local designers, craftspeople and artists, whose boutiques and workshops lend La Ribera an air of creativity. Galleries and applied art museums occupy the medieval mansions of Carrer de Montcada – the neighbourhood's most handsome street – while the *barri* is at its most hip in the area around the Passeig del Born, whose cafés, restaurants and bars are especially lively at night. The most direct access point for La Ribera is Metro Jaume I.

Museu Picasso

MAP P.70, POCKET MAP F13.
C/de Montcada 15–23. Ⓜ Jaume. I
Ⓦ museupicasso.bcn.cat. Charge, free for under-18s, first Sun of the month & Thurs 5–7pm.

The celebrated Museu Picasso is one of the most important collections of Picasso's work in the world, but even so, some visitors are disappointed, since the museum chronicles his time living in the city and therefore contains few of his best-known pictures and not many in the Cubist style. But there are almost 4000 works

Museu Picasso

in the permanent collection – housed in five adjoining medieval palaces – and these provide a fascinating opportunity to trace his development.

Paintings from his art-school days in Barcelona (1895–97) show tantalizing glimpses of the city that the young Picasso was beginning to explore, while works in the style of Toulouse-Lautrec reflect his interest in Parisian art. Other selected works are from the famous Blue Period (1901–04) and Pink Period (1904–06), and from his Cubist (1907–20) and Neoclassical (1920–25) stages. The large gaps in the main collection only underline Picasso's extraordinary changes of style and mood, best illustrated by the jump to 1957, a year represented by his interpretations of Velázquez's masterpiece *Las Meninas*. As well as showing changing selections of sketches, prints and drawings, the museum addresses Picasso's work as a ceramicist, highlighting the vibrantly decorated dishes and jugs donated by his wife Jacqueline.

A guided tour is the best way to get to grips with the collection (in English on Tues, Sat and Sun, extra charge, book in advance by

Basílica de Santa María del Mar

phone or via the website). There's a courtyard café, and, of course, a shop full of Picasso-related gifts.

Museu Europeu d'Art Modern

MAP P.70, POCKET MAP F13.
C/Barra de Ferro 5. ⓂJaume I. Ⓦmeam.es.
Charge, extra for guided tour.

There is not one photograph on display at the Museu Europeu d'Art Modern, a fact you may

Picasso in Barcelona

Although born in Málaga, **Pablo Picasso** (1881–1973) spent much of his youth – from the age of 14 to 23 – in Barcelona. This time encompassed the whole of his Blue Period (1901–04) and provided many of the formative influences on his art. Not far from the Museu Picasso you can see many of the buildings in which Picasso lived and worked, notably the Escola de Belles Arts de Llotja (C/Consolat del Mar, near Estació de França), where his father taught drawing and where Picasso himself absorbed an academic training. The apartments where the family lived when they first arrived in Barcelona were at Pg. d'Isabel II 4 and C/Reina Cristina 3, both near the Escola, while Picasso's first real studio (in 1896) was located over on C/de la Plata at no. 4. A few years later, many of his Blue Period works were finished at a studio at C/del Comerç 28. His first public exhibition was in 1901 at the extravagantly decorated *Els Quatre Gats* tavern (see page 41) in Barri Gòtic; you can still have a meal there today.

find hard to believe considering how photorealistic many of the paintings are. Located in a renovated eighteenth-century palace – and just metres from the Museu Picasso – the museum focuses on contemporary figurative art. Its three floors brim with haunting, humorous and sometimes disturbing works by the likes of Eduardo Naranjo, Paul Beel and Carlos Saura Riaza. It's also home to modern, Art Deco and Catalan sculptures.

Basílica de Santa María del Mar

MAP P.70, POCKET MAP F13.
Pl. de Santa Maria. Ⓜ Jaume I.
Ⓦ santamariadelmarbarcelona.org.
Free, charge for guided tours (in English Fri–Sun).

The Ribera's flagship church is perhaps the most beautiful in all Barcelona. It was begun on the order of King Jaume II in 1324, and finished in just 55 years.

Built on what was the seashore in the fourteenth century, Santa María was at the centre of the medieval city's trading district (nearby Carrer de l'Argentería, for example, is named after the silversmiths who once worked there), and it came to embody the commercial supremacy of the Crown of Aragon, of which Barcelona was capital. It's an exquisite example of Catalan-Gothic architecture – as all the later Baroque trappings were destroyed during the Civil War, eyes instead are concentrated on the simple spaces of the interior, especially the stained glass. Check local listings magazines for choral concerts here – the acoustics are as stunning as the architecture.

Passeig del Born

MAP P.70, POCKET MAP F13.
Ⓜ Jaume I.

Running from the back of the church of Santa María del Mar

is the fashionable Passeig del Born, once the site of medieval fairs and entertainments ("born" means tournament) and now an avenue lined with a parade of plane trees shading a host of classy bars, delis and shops. At night the Born becomes one of Barcelona's biggest bar zones, as spirited locals frequent a panoply of drinking haunts – from old-style cocktail lounges to thumping music bars. Shoppers and browsers, meanwhile, scour the narrow medieval alleys on either side of the *passeig* for boutiques and craft workshops – Carrers Flassaders, Vidrieria and Rec, in particular, are noted for clothes, shoes, jewellery and design galleries.

El Born Centre de Cultura i Memòria

MAP P.70, POCKET MAP G13.
Pl. Comercial 12. Ⓜ Jaume I/Barceloneta.
Ⓦ elborncentrecultural.cat. Free, charge for guided tours.

The Antic Mercat del Born (1873–76) was the biggest of Barcelona's nineteenth-century market halls. It was the city's main wholesale fruit and veg market in 1971, and was then due to be demolished, but was saved thanks to local protests. It lay empty for decades, but in 2013 reopened as El Born Centre de Cultura i Memòria; the extensive archeological remains of eighteenth-century shops, factories, houses and taverns are showcased inside the building's restored glass-and-cast-iron frame.

Museu de Cultures del Món

MAP P.70, POCKET MAP E13.
C/Montcada 12–14. Ⓜ Jaume I.
Ⓦ museuculturesmon.bcn.cat. Charge.
The Museum of World Cultures in the Palau Nadal and Palau Marqués de Lliö brings together archeological collections from around the world that show the diversity of global art throughout history.

The Antic Mercat del Born

Shops

Almacen Marabi

MAP P.70, POCKET MAP F13.
C/Cirera 6. Ⓜ Jaume I.
Ⓦ almacenmarabi.blogspot.com.
Mariela Marabi, originally from
Argentina, makes handmade felt
finger dolls, mobiles, puppets
and animals of extraordinary
invention. She's often at work at
the back, while her eye-popping
showroom also has limited-edition
pieces by other selected artists and
designers.

La Botifarreria de Santa Maria

MAP P.70, POCKET MAP F14.
C/Santa Maria 4. Ⓜ Jaume I.
Ⓦ labotifarreria.com.
If you ever doubted the power of
the humble Catalan pork sausage,
drop by this designer temple-
deli where otherwise beautifully
behaved locals jostle at the
counter for the day's home-made
botifarra, plus rigorously sourced
hams, cheese, pâtés and salamis.
True disciples can even buy the
T-shirt.

Bubó

MAP P.70, POCKET MAP E14.
C/Caputxes 10. Ⓜ Jaume I. Ⓦ bubo.es.
There are chocolates and then
there are Bubó chocolates – jewel-
like creations and playful desserts
by pastry maestro Carles Mampel.
There's also a coffee machine and
a handful of seats if you want to
sample the cakes in-store.

La Campana

MAP P.70, POCKET MAP F13.
C/Princesa 36. Ⓜ Jaume I.
Ⓦ lacampanadesde1890.com.
This lovely old shop from 1890
presents handmade pralines and
truffles, but is best known for
its beautifully packaged squares
and slabs of *turrón*, traditional
Catalan nougat.

Casa Gispert

Casa Gispert

MAP P.70, POCKET MAP F13.
C/Sombrerers 23. Ⓜ Jaume I.
Ⓦ casagispert.com.

Roasters of nuts, coffee and spices since 1851. It's a truly delectable store of wooden boxes, baskets, stacked shelves and tantalizing smells, and there are organic nuts and dried fruit, teas and gourmet deli items available too.

Custo Barcelona

MAP P.70, POCKET MAP F14.
Pl. de les Olles 7. Ⓜ Barceloneta.
Ⓦ custo.com.

Where the stars get their T-shirts – hugely colourful (highly-priced) designer tops and sweaters for men and women. There's another store, where last season's gear gets another whirl, at Plaça del Pi in the Barri Gòtic.

Iriarte Iriarte

MAP P.70, POCKET MAP E13.
C/Rera Palau 2. Ⓜ Jaume I.
Ⓦ iriarteiriarte.com.

Atelier-showroom for sumptuous handmade leather bags and belts. The area also has several other interesting craft workshops and galleries to browse.

Vila Viniteca

MAP P.70, POCKET MAP E14.
C/Agullers 7 & 9. Ⓜ Jaume I.
Ⓦ vilaviniteca.es.

A very knowledgeable specialist in Catalan and Spanish wines. Pick your vintage and then nip over the road for the gourmet deli part of the operation.

Cafés

Demasié

MAP P.70, POCKET MAP G13.
C/de la Princesa 28. Ⓜ Jaume I.
Ⓦ cookiesdemasie.com.

For those with a sweet tooth, this is the perfect place to begin your day or have a snack in between sightseeing. A cosy café offering

Custo Barcelona

mouth-watering cinnamon rolls and various types of cookies, cupcakes and cakes. €

Llamber

MAP P.70, POCKET MAP G13.
C/de la Fusina 5. Ⓜ Jaume I.
Ⓦ llamber.com.

A modern factory of first-rate Asturian tapas in a former industrial warehouse facing the Mercat del Born cultural centre. There are full dishes, such as quail with garlic and octopus with creamed potato, but the emphasis is very much on eating and drinking in groups. €

Restaurants and tapas bars

Cal Pep

MAP P.70, POCKET MAP F14.
Pl. de les Olles 8. Ⓜ Barceloneta.
Ⓦ calpep.com.

There's no equal in town for off-the-boat and out-of-the-market tapas. You may have to queue, and prices are high for what's effectively a bar meal, but it's definitely worth it for the likes of impeccably fried shrimp, grilled sea bass, Catalan sausage, or squid and chickpeas – all overseen by Pep himself, bustling up and down the counter. €€€

Carmina

MAP P.70, POCKET MAP E13.
C/Argenteria 37. Ⓜ Jaume I.
Ⓦ carminarestaurante.com.

A gorgeous renovation of an eighteenth-century building has been artfully blended with neon, artsy ceramics and oversized lamps and is now the home of *Carmina*. The speciality is superb Italian food with nods to Spanish cuisine, such as oxtail croquettes with pecorino, and the pasta dishes are especially good. €€

Euskal Etxea

MAP P.70, POCKET MAP F13.
Pl. de Montcada 1–3. Ⓜ Jaume I.
Ⓦ gruposagardi.com.

The bar at the front of the local Basque community centre is great for sampling *pintxos* – elaborately fashioned tapas held together by a cocktail stick. Just point to what

you want – and keep the sticks so the bill can be tallied. €€

The Pan's Club

MAP P.70, POCKET MAP F13.
Pl.de la Llana 16. Ⓜ Jaume I.
Ⓦ thepansclub.com.

A small place full to the brim of healthy vegetarian dishes made from local produce. Amazing quiche and a great selection of salads, you can also grab a sandwich or a bagel to go and follow it with an excellent smoothie. €

Pim Pam Burger

MAP P.70, POCKET MAP F13.
C/Sabateret 4. Ⓜ Jaume I.
Ⓦ pimpamburger.com.

An acceptable choice for a quick burger, hot dog or sandwich. There are a few stools and tables if you'd rather not eat on the hoof, while *Pim Pam Plats*, around the corner on C/del Rec, is their outlet for budget-beating take-home meals.

El Xampanyet

MAP P.70, POCKET MAP F13.
C/de Montcada 22. Ⓜ Jaume I.
☎ 933 197 003.

La Botifarreria de Santa María

Chocolate cake at Bubó

Traditional blue-tiled bar doing a roaring trade in sparkling cava, cider and traditional tapas (anchovies are the speciality). The drinks are cheap and the tapas turn out to be rather pricey, but there's usually a good buzz about the place. €

Bars

Espai Barroc

MAP P.70, POCKET MAP F13.
Palau Dalmases, C/de Montcada 20.
Ⓜ Jaume I. Ⓦ eventospalaudalmases.com.
The handsome Baroque mansion of Palau Dalmases is open in the evenings for wine, champagne or cognac in refined surroundings, along with occasional flamenco shows (see website for details).

Marlowe

MAP P.70, POCKET MAP F14.
C/del Rec 24. Ⓜ Barceloneta.
Ⓦ marlowe.bar.
A slightly noir atmosphere in this small, elegant cocktail bar – yes, the bar is named after the famous

Chandlerian character. There is no set drink menu, just talk to the creative bartenders and their professional hands will mix something just for you.

Mudanzas

MAP P.70, POCKET MAP F14.
C/Vidriería 15. Ⓜ Barceloneta.
Ⓦ barmudanzas.com.
A recent change in ownership means that this much beloved local haunt is now popular with a young, international cocktail crowd, but during the day it's still a relatively peaceful place for a beer off the main drag.

La Vinya del Senyor

MAP P.70, POCKET MAP F14.
Pl. Santa Maria 5. Ⓜ Jaume I.
Ⓦ lavinyadelsenyor.es.
A great wine bar with front-row seats onto the lovely church of Santa María del Mar. The wine list is really good – with a score available by the glass – and there are oysters, smoked salmon and other classy tapas available.

Parc de la Ciutadella

While you might escape to Montjuïc or the Collserola hills for the air, there's no beating the city's green lung, Parc de la Ciutadella, for a break from the downtown bustle. Though the park holds a full set of attractions, on lazy summer days you may simply want to stroll along the garden paths and row lazily across the ornamental lake. The name of the park recalls a Bourbon citadel which used to occupy the site, the building of which caused the brutal destruction of a great part of La Ribera neighbourhood. This symbol of authority survived uneasily until 1869; after this the area was made into a park. It was subsequently chosen as the site of the 1888 Universal Exhibition, from which period dates a series of eye-catching buildings and monuments by the city's pioneering *modernista* architects.

Arc de Triomf

MAP P.77, POCKET MAP G11.
Pg. Lluís Companys. ⓦ Arc de Triomf.
A giant brick arch announces the architectural splendours to come in the park itself. Conceived as a bold statement of Catalan intent, it's studded with ceramic figures and motifs and topped by two pairs of bulbous domes. The reliefs on the main facade show the City of Barcelona welcoming visitors to the

Cascada, Parc de la Ciutadella

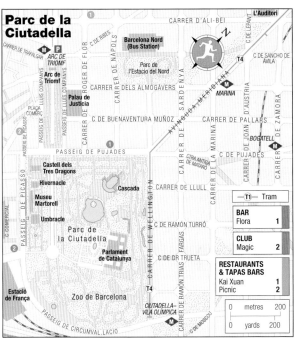

Parc de la Ciutadella

1888 Universal Exhibition, held in the park to the south. Connecting the arch to the park is a gorgeous promenade flanked by linden and palm trees and ornate lamp posts. Just before the park's entrance on Passeig de Pujades stands the monument to Francisco de Paula Rius i Taulet, the four-time mayor of Barcelona credited with helping bring the Universal Exhibition to the city.

Cascada
MAP P.77, POCKET MAP K6.
Parc de la Ciutadella. Ⓜ Arc de Triomf.
The first of the major projects undertaken inside the park was the Cascada, the monumental fountain in the northeast corner. It was designed by Josep Fontseré i Mestrès, the architect chosen to oversee the conversion of the former citadel grounds into a park, and his assistant was the young Antoni Gaudí, then a student. The Baroque

extravagance of the Cascada is suggestive of the flamboyant decoration that was later to become Gaudí's trademark. The best place to contemplate the fountain is from the small open-air café-kiosk. Near here you'll also find a small lake, where you can rent a rowing boat and paddle about among the ducks.

Hivernacle and Umbracle
MAP P.77, POCKET MAP G13.
Pg. de Picasso. Ⓜ Arc de Triomf. Free.
The two unsung glories of Ciutadella are its plant houses, arranged either side of the Museu Martorell. The larger Hivernacle (conservatory) features enclosed greenhouses separated by a soaring glass-roofed terrace, however, at the time of writing, it was closed for renovation. If anything, the Umbracle (palmhouse) is even more imposing, with a vaulted wood-slat roof supported by cast-iron pillars, which allows shafts of

Zoo de Barcelona

light to play across the assembled palms and ferns. Traditionally, there's always been a café-bar in the Hivernacle, set among the plants and trees, though it has been closed for a few years, but the renovations should see it reopen in 2024.

Museu de Ciències Naturals

MAP P.77, POCKET MAP G12 & G13. Pg. de Picasso. Ⓜ Arc de Triomf. Ⓦ museuciencies.bcn.cat.

The city's Natural Science Museum has its public showcase, the Museu Blau, over at the Diagonal Mar Fòrum site, but its genesis lies in two interesting buildings in Ciutadella park that are currently undergoing major renovation (and will be for some time). The Neoclassical **Museu Martorell**, which opened in 1882, was actually the first public museum to be built in the city, designed by leading architect of the day Antoni Rovira i Trias. For decades this housed the city's geological collections;

the new permanent exhibition here will concentrate on the relationship between humans and nature. The other building has always been a city favourite, a whimsical red-brick confection that was long the zoology museum. It's universally known as the **Castell dels Tres Dragons** (Three Dragons Castle), designed by *modernista* architect Lluís Domènech i Montaner and originally intended for use as the café-restaurant for the 1888 Universal Exhibition. It's going to become the research, study and conservation centre for the Natural Science Museum's geology and zoology collections, and will be known as the Laboratori de Natura (Laboratory of Nature).

Zoo de Barcelona

MAP P.77, POCKET MAP J7–K7. C/de Wellington. Ⓜ Ciutadella-Vila Olímpica. Ⓦ zoobarcelona.cat. Charge. Ciutadella's most popular attraction by far is the city zoo, which takes up most of the southeastern part of the park (main entrance on Carrer de Wellington, signposted from Ⓜ Ciutadella-Vila Olímpica). It has more than 2000 animals from over 300 different species – which is seen by some as too many for a zoo that is still essentially nineteenth century in character, confined to the formal grounds of a public park. Nonetheless it's hugely popular with families, as there are mini-train and pony rides and a petting zoo alongside the main animal attractions. The many endangered species on show include the Iberian wolf, and big cats such as the Sri Lankan leopard, snow leopard and the Sumatran tiger. The zoo's days in its current form are numbered: over the next few years parts of it will be completely remodelled as it attempts to expand its facilities and modernize.

Restaurants and tapas bars

Kai Xuan

MAP P.77, POCKET MAP J5.
C/Roger de Flor 74. Ⓜ Arc de Triomf.
☎ 932 450 359.

Forget El Raval's so-called Barrio Xinès, the city's real Chinatown is in the streets near this family restaurant. Specializing in hand-pulled *lamian* noodles and pan-fried dumplings, *Kai Xuan* fills up fast every day with Chinese people and in-the-know locals. €

Picnic

MAP P.77, POCKET MAP G12.
C/Comerç 1. Ⓜ Arc de Triomf.
Ⓦ bit.ly/PicnicBarcelona.

Just a short stroll from the park, this lovely little spot serves classic brunch food (Fri–Sun) such as eggs Benedict, pancakes and French toast, plus more creative dishes like duck hash and fried green tomatoes. The dinner menu focuses on tapas, with offerings that include oysters in tempura, grilled kangaroo and Myanmar pickled tea-leaf salad. There's also a weekday lunch menu (Tues–Thurs), as well as thirst-quenching drinks such as the refreshingly tart pink lemonade. €€

Bar

Flora

MAP P.77, POCKET MAP C11.
Passeig Pujades 21. Ⓜ Arc de Triomf.
Ⓦ instagram.com/floracafebcn.

Start a morning wandering around Barcelona's loveliest park with brunch at one of Flora's terrace tables. Eggs benedict, avocado toast and all the breakfast favourites are available, along with freshly squeezed juices, excellent coffee and fun, friendly waiters.

Club

Magic

MAP P.77, POCKET MAP G13.
Pg. Picasso 40. Ⓜ Barceloneta. Ⓦ magic-club.net.

A Barcelona classic that's been rocking out since the mid-1970s. While first and foremost a rock 'n' roll club, *Magic* doesn't take itself too seriously. The usual suspects (Ramones, AC/DC and Iggy Pop) are played alongside hits from the likes of the Beastie Boys, the Violent Femmes and more.

Picnic

PARC DE LA CIUTADELLA

Montjuïc

For art and gardens you need to head across the city to the verdant park area of Montjuïc, site of the 1992 Olympics. The hill is topped by a sturdy castle and anchored around the heavyweight art collections in the Museu Nacional d'Art de Catalunya (MNAC). Two other superb galleries also draw visitors, namely CaixaForum and the celebrated Fundació Joan Miró, not to mention a whole host of family-oriented attractions, from the open-air Poble Espanyol (Spanish Village) to the cable car ride to the castle. Meanwhile, the various gardens that spill down the hillsides culminate in Barcelona's excellent botanical gardens. For CaixaForum, Poble Espanyol and MNAC use Metro Espanya; the Telefèric del Port (cable car from Barceloneta) and Funicular de Montjuïc (from Metro Paral·lel) drop you near the Fundació Joan Miró. At the bottom of the hill is Poble Sec, mostly residential but with an increasing number of bars and restaurants, particularly along the pedestrianised strip of Carrer de Blai. Across the broad Avinguda Paral·lel is the district of Sant Antoni, which in recent years has become the coolest in town for quirky shops, wine bars, superb restaurants and hip cafés. At its heart is the nineteenth-century Mercat Sant Antoni, which had a glittering revamp in 2018.

Plaça d'Espanya

Plaça d'Espanya

MAP P.81, POCKET MAP C4.
Ⓜ Espanya.

Montjuïc's characteristic gardens, terraces, fountains and monumental buildings were established for the International Exhibition of 1929. Gateway to the Exhibition was the vast Plaça d'Espanya and its huge Neoclassical fountain, with striking twin towers, 47m high, standing at the foot of the imposing Avinguda de la Reina Maria Cristina. This avenue heads up towards Montjuïc, and is lined by exhibition halls used for trade fairs. At the end, monumental steps (and modern escalators) ascend the hill to the Palau Nacional (home of MNAC), past water cascades and under the flanking walls of two grand Viennese-style pavilions. The

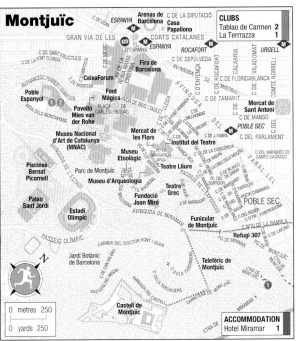

higher you climb, the better the views, while a few café-kiosks put out seats on the way up to MNAC.

Monument de les Quatre Columnes

MAP P.81, POCKET MAP C4.
Ⓜ Espanya.

The simplest of architect Josep Puig i Cadafalch's ideas for the ceremonial gateway to Montjuïc at Plaça d'Espanya were four 20m-high columns, erected in 1919 on a raised site below the future Palau Nacional. Who could possibly object? The authoritarian government of General Primo de Rivera, as it happened, knowing perfectly well that the architect, a Catalan nationalist, meant the four columns to represent the four stripes of the Catalan flag. Down they came in 1928, to be replaced by the Magic Fountain, and not until 2010 were the columns reconstructed (using the original plans) to be seen again in public – erected across from the fountain by the city government as "an act of memory" and symbol of freedom and democracy.

CaixaForum

MAP P.81, POCKET MAP C4.
Av. Francesc Ferrer i Guàrdia 6–8.
Ⓜ Espanya. Ⓦ bit.ly/CaixaBarc. Charge.

The former Casaramona textile factory (1911) at the foot of Montjuïc conceals a terrific arts and cultural centre. The exhibition halls were fashioned from the former factory buildings, whose external structure was left untouched – girders, pillars, brickwork and crenellated walls appear at every turn. The undulating roof (signposted "terrats") offers unique views, while the high Casaramona tower, etched in blue and yellow tiling, is as readily recognizable as the huge Miró starfish logos emblazoned across the building.

Poble Espanyol open-air architectural museum

The contemporary art collection focuses on the period from the 1980s to the present, and works are shown in partial rotation alongside an excellent programme of changing exhibitions across all aspects of the arts. There's also the Mediateca multimedia space, plus an arts bookshop, children's activities and a 400-seat auditorium for music, art and literary events.

Font Màgica

MAP P.81, POCKET MAP C5.
Pl. de Carles Buigas Ⓜ Espanya.
Ⓦ bit.ly/FontMagicaBarc. Free.
On selected evenings, the "Magic Fountain" at the foot of the Montjuïc steps becomes the centrepiece of an impressive, if slightly kitsch, sound-and-light show, as the sprays and sheets of brightly coloured water dance to the music. A severe drought in Spain saw the city's fountains turned off for most of 2023 – check the website for updated information.

Pavelló Mies van der Rohe

MAP P.81, POCKET MAP C5.
Av. Francesc Ferrer i Guàrdia 7. Ⓜ Espanya.
Ⓦ miesbcn.com. Charge.

The German contribution to the 1929 International Exhibition was a pavilion designed by Mies van der Rohe (and reconstructed in 1986 by Catalan architects). It's considered a major example of modern rationalist architecture – a startling conjunction of dark-green polished onyx, shining glass and watery surfaces. Unless there's an exhibition in place (a fairly regular occurrence) there is little to see inside, though you can buy postcards and books from the small shop and debate quite how much you want a "Less is More" T-shirt.

Poble Espanyol

MAP P.81, POCKET MAP B5.
Av. Francesc Ferrer i Guàrdia 13.
Ⓜ Espanya. Ⓦ poble-espanyol.com.
Charge.

"Get to know Spain in one hour" is what's promised at the Spanish Village – an open-air park of reconstructed Spanish buildings, such as the medieval walls of Ávila, through which you enter. The echoing main square is lined with cafés, while the surrounding streets and alleys contain around forty workshops, where you can witness crafts like engraving, weaving and pottery. Inevitably, it's one huge shopping experience, and prices are inflated, but children will love it (they can run free as there's no traffic) and there are plenty of family activities. Get to the village early to enjoy it in relatively crowd-free circumstances – once the tour groups arrive, it becomes a bit of a scrum. You could always come instead at the other end of the day, to venues like *Tablao de Carmen* or *La Terrrazza*, when the village transforms into a vibrant centre of Barcelona nightlife.

Museu de Carrosses Fúnebres

MAP P.81, POCKET MAP A8.
C/Mare de Déu de Port 56–58. Bus #21 from Ⓜ Paral·lel. Ⓦ cbsa.cat. Free.
One of the city's more esoteric attractions, the Funerary Carriage Museum is fittingly located at the entrance to Montjuïc cemetery. The horse-drawn carriages on display were used for city funeral processions from the 1830s until the service was mechanized in the 1950s, when the silver Buick (also on display) came into use. Most of the carriages and hearses are extravagantly decorated, and some carried dignitaries, politicians and big-name bullfighters to their final resting places. There are also plenty of old photographs of them in use in the city's streets, alongside antique uniforms, mourning wear and formal riding gear.

Museu Nacional d'Art de Catalunya (MNAC)

MAP P.81, POCKET MAP C5/6.
Palau Nacional. Ⓜ Espanya.
Ⓦ museunacional.cat. Charge, free every Sat from 3pm and first Sun of the month.
Catalunya's national art gallery is one of Barcelona's essential visits, showcasing a thousand years of Catalan art in stupendous surroundings. For first-time visitors

it can be difficult to know where to start, but if time is limited it's recommended you concentrate on the medieval collection. It's split into two main sections, one dedicated to Romanesque art and the other to Gothic – periods in which Catalunya's artists were pre-eminent in Spain.

The collection of Romanesque frescoes in particular is the museum's pride and joy – removed from churches in the Catalan Pyrenees, and presented in a reconstruction of their original setting. MNAC also boasts an unsurpassed nineteenth- and twentieth-century Catalan art collection (until the 1940s – everything from the 1950s onwards is covered by MACBA in El Raval). It's particularly strong on *modernista* and *noucentista* painting and sculpture, the two dominant schools of the period, while there are some fascinating diversions into subjects like *modernista* interior design, avant-garde sculpture and historical photography.

Blockbuster exhibitions, and special shows based on the

Museu Nacional d'Art de Catalunya

museum's archives are popular (separate charges may apply).

Museu Etnològic

MAP P.81, POCKET MAP C6.
Pg. Santa Madrona 16–22. Ⓜ Espanya.
Ⓦ bit.ly/MuseuEtno. Charge.

The Ethnological Museum boasts extensive global cultural collections and puts on excellent exhibitions, which usually last for a year or two and focus on a particular subject or geographical area. Refreshingly, pieces close to home aren't neglected, which means that there's also often a focus on local and national themes, such as rural life and work or Spanish carnival celebrations.

Museu d'Arqueologia

MAP P.81, POCKET MAP C6.
Pg. Santa Madrona 39–41. Ⓜ Espanya.
Ⓦ mac.cat. Charge.

The city's main archeological collection spans the centuries from

the Stone Age to the time of the Visigoths, with the Roman and Greek periods particularly well represented. Finds from Catalunya's best-preserved archeological site – the Greek remains at Empúries on the Costa Brava – are notable, while on an upper floor life in Barcino (Roman Barcelona) is interpreted through a vivid array of tombstones, statues, inscriptions and friezes.

La Ciutat del Teatre

MAP P.81, POCKET MAP C5–D6.
Mercat de les Flors Ⓜ Poble Sec.
Ⓦ mercatflors.cat. Teatre Lliure
Ⓦ teatrelliure.cat. Institut del Teatre
Ⓦ teatrelliure.cat.

At the foot of Montjuïc the theatre area known as La Ciutat del Teatre ("Theatre City") occupies a corner of the old working-class neighbourhood of Poble Sec. Here, off Carrer de Lleida, you'll find the **Mercat de les Flors** – once a flower

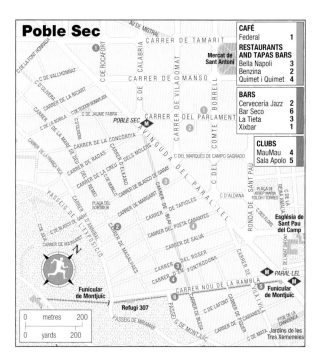

La Ciutat del Teatre

market, now a centre for dance and the "movement arts" – and the progressive **Teatre Lliure** ("Free Theatre"), while the sleek **Institut del Teatre** brings together the city's major drama and dance schools.

Poble Sec

MAP P.84, POCKET MAP D5–E6.
Ⓜ Poble Sec.

The Poble Sec neighbourhood provides a complete contrast to the landscaped slopes of Montjuïc. The name ("Dry Village") is derived from the fact that this working-class neighbourhood originally had no water supply. Today, the hillside grid of streets is lined with down-to-earth grocery stores and good-value restaurants, while it

is also emerging as an "off-Raval" nightlife destination, with its fashionable bars and music clubs – pedestrianized Carrer de Blai is the epicentre of the scene. It has its own metro station, or it's an easy walk from El Raval, while the Montjuïc funicular has its lower station at nearby Ⓜ Paral·lel.

Refugi 307

MAP P.84, POCKET MAP D7/8.
C/Nou de la Rambla 175. Ⓜ Paral·lel.
Ⓦ museuhistoria.bcn.cat. Charge.

For a fascinating look at one of the city's hidden corners, visit Poble Sec's old Civil War air-raid shelter, dug into the hillside by local people in 1936. The tunnels could shelter up to 2000 people

Teatre Grec and the Barcelona Festival

Centrepiece of Barcelona's annual summer cultural festival (Ⓦ grec.bcn.cat) is the **Teatre Grec** (Greek Theatre), cut into a former quarry on the Montjuïc hillside. Starting in late June (and running throughout July and sometimes early Aug), the festival incorporates drama, music and dance, with some of the most atmospheric events staged in the Greek theatre, from Shakespearean productions to shows by avant-garde performance artists.

from Franco's bombs – you follow your guide into the labyrinth to the sound of screaming sirens, which at the time gave the locals just two minutes to get safely underground. Storyboards and photographs by the entrance explain the gripping history of the Civil War in Barcelona. Tours are in Spanish or Catalan, though someone usually speaks English, and you can just turn up on the day.

Estadi Olímpic

MAP P.81, POCKET MAP B6.
Museu Olímpic i de l'Esport, Av. de l'Estadi 60. Ⓜ Espanya. Ⓦ museuolimpicbcn.cat. Charge.

The 65,000-seater Olympic Stadium was the ceremonial venue for the 1992 Barcelona Olympics. From the front, a vast *terrassa* provides one of the finest vantage points in the city, while the space-age curve of Santiago Calatrava's communications tower dominates the skyline.

Around the other side, across the road from the stadium, the history of the Games – and Barcelona's successful hosting – are covered in the Olympic and Sports Museum.

It's a fully interactive experience, with lots of sports gear and memorabilia displayed, but even so it's probably one for hardcore Olympics fans only.

Fundació Joan Miró

MAP P.81, POCKET MAP C6.
Parc de Montjuïc. Ⓜ Espanya. Ⓦ fmirobcn.org. Charge.

Barcelona's most adventurous art museum houses the life's work of the great Catalan artist Joan Miró (1893–1983). Inside the stark white building is a permanent collection of works largely donated by Miró himself and covering the period from 1914 to 1978. The paintings and drawings in particular are instantly recognizable, being among the chief links between Surrealism and abstract art, while there's also a selection of fascinating original sketches – Miró's enormous tapestries and outdoor sculptures, for example, often started life as a doodle on a scrap of notepaper. The museum's Sala K provides a rapid appraisal of Miró's entire *oeuvre* in a representative selection of works. Elsewhere are pieces

Fundació Joan Miró

by other artists in homage to Miró, and exhibitions by young experimental artists in the Espai 13 gallery.

The museum sponsors temporary exhibitions, film shows, lectures and children's theatre. There's also a café-restaurant with outdoor tables on a sunny patio – and you don't need a museum ticket to go in.

Funicular de Montjuïc

MAP P.84, POCKET MAP D6.
Av. del Paral·lel. Ⓜ Paral·lel. Ⓦ tmb.cat.
Charge.

The quickest way to reach the lower heights of Montjuïc is to take the funicular, from inside the station at Ⓜ Paral·lel. At the upper station you can switch to the Montjuïc cable car, or you're only a few minutes' walk from the Fundació Joan Miró.

Telefèric de Montjuïc

MAP P.81, POCKET MAP D7.
Av. de Miramar. Ⓜ Paral·lel, then Funicular.
Ⓦ tmb.cat. Charge.

The cable car up to the castle and back is an exciting ride, and the views, of course, are stupendous. There's an intermediate station, called Mirador, where you can get out and enjoy more sweeping vistas.

Castell de Montjuïc

MAP P.81, POCKET MAP C7/8.
Carretera de Montjuïc.
Ⓦ bcn.cat/castelldemontjuic. Charge.

Barcelona's fortress served as a military base and prison for decades, and was where the last president of the pre-war Catalan government, Lluís Companys, was executed on Franco's orders on October 15, 1940. However, in 2008 the castle was symbolically handed over to the city and its various spaces can now be visited. Exhibitions explain the history of the fortress, and the cable car ride and dramatic location merit a visit in their own right. The rampart views are magnificent, while

Jardí Botànic de Barcelona

below the walls the panoramic **Camí del Mar** pathway looks out over the port and ocean. It runs for one kilometre to the Mirador del Migdia viewpoint, where there's a great open-air bar called *La Caseta* (weekends from noon, plus summer weekend DJ nights).

Jardí Botànic de Barcelona

MAP P.81, POCKET MAP B7.
C/Dr Font i Quer 2. Ⓜ Espanya.
Ⓦ museuciencies.bcn.cat. Charge, combined ticket with Museu Blau (Museu de Ciències Naturals) available, free first Sun of the month and every Sun from 3pm.

Principal among Montjuïc's many gardens is the city's Botanical Garden, laid out on terraced slopes offering fine views over the city. The Montjuïc buses run here directly, or it's a five-minute walk around the back of the Olympic Stadium. The beautifully kept contemporary garden has landscaped zones representing the flora of the Mediterranean, Canary Islands, California, Chile, South Africa and Australia. Just try to avoid arriving in the full heat of a summer day, as there's very little shade.

Café

Federal

MAP P.84, POCKET MAP E5.
C/del Parlament 39. Ⓜ Sant Antoni.
Ⓦ federalcafe.es.

Australian-style brunch has broken into Barcelona via this cosy corner café with a great little roof garden. Whether you're looking for a flat white and French toast, a bacon butty and a glass of New Zealand Sauvignon Blanc or a dandelion soy latte, you can guarantee that there's nowhere else quite like this in town. €

Restaurants and tapas bars

Bella Napoli

MAP P.84, POCKET MAP E6.
C/Margarit 14. Ⓜ Poble Sec.
Ⓦ bellanapoli.es.

Authentic Neapolitan pizzeria serving some of the city's finest pizzas straight from a beehive-shaped oven. Or there's a huge

Quimet i Quimet

range of pastas, risottos and veal *scaloppine*. €€

Benzina

MAP P.84, POCKET MAP E5.
Passatge de Pere Calders 6. Ⓜ Poble Sec.
Ⓦ benzina.es.

Down a wide pedestrianised alleyway off the hipster drag of Carrer del Parlament is this industrially chic Italian restaurant, serving some of the best food around. The convivial atmosphere and upbeat seventies and eighties soundtrack provide a joyful backdrop to *linguine aglio e olio* with lobster and avocado, a heavenly carbonara and much more. €€€

Quimet i Quimet

MAP P.84, POCKET MAP E6.
C/Poeta Cabanyes 25. Ⓜ Paral·lel.
Ⓦ quimetiquimet.

Poble Sec's cosiest tapas bar is a place of pilgrimage where classy finger food is served from a minuscule counter. €€

Bars

Cervecería Jazz

MAP P.84, POCKET MAP D6.
C/Margarit 43. Ⓜ Poble Sec.
Ⓦ cerveceriajazz.com.

Grab a stool at the carved bar and shoot the breeze over a Catalan craft beer. It's an amiable joint with great music, from jazz to reggae, and locals swear that the burgers are the best in town.

Bar Seco

MAP P.84, POCKET MAP E6.
Pg. Montjuïc 74. Ⓜ Paral·lel. ☎ 933 296 374.
The "Dry Bar" is a local hit, with its mellow vibe, fresh juices and artisan beers. It was one of the first places in Barcelona to embrace the Slow Food movement.

La Tieta

MAP P.84, POCKET MAP E6.
C/de Blai 1. Ⓜ Paral·lel.

Sala Apolo

Ⓦ bodegalatieta.com.
Small but perfectly formed, "The
Aunt" is a cool drinks and tapas
place with an open window onto
the street and just enough room for
a dozen or so good friends.

Xixbar

MAP P.84, POCKET MAP D5.
C/Rocafort 19. Ⓜ Poble Sec. Ⓦ xixbar.com.
An old *granja* (milk bar) turned
candlelit cocktail bar. It's big on gin,
boasting over a hundred varieties.

Clubs

MauMau

MAP P.84, POCKET MAP E6.
C/Fontrodona 33. Ⓜ Paral·lel.
Ⓦ maumaunderground.com.
Underground lounge-club, cultural
centre and chill-out space, with
nightly video projections, all
sorts of exhibitions and guest DJs
playing deep, soulful grooves.

Sala Apolo

MAP P.84, POCKET MAP A13.
C/Nou de la Rambla 113. Ⓜ Paral·lel.
Ⓦ sala-apolo.com.

Old-time ballroom turned hip
concert venue with gigs on two
stages (local acts to big names) and
an eclectic series of club nights,
from punk or Catalan rumba
sounds to the weekend's long-
running *Nitsa Club* (Ⓦ nitsa.com).
Entry charges vary.

Tablao de Carmen

MAP P.81, POCKET MAP B5.
Poble Espanyol. Ⓜ Espanya.
Ⓦ tablaodecarmen.com.
Poble Espanyol's famous flamenco
club features a variety of shows
twice a night from seasoned
performers and new talent.
Tickets start from simple ones for
the show and a drink, through
to inclusive of tapas or dinner.
Reservations required.

La Terrrazza

MAP P.81, POCKET MAP B5.
Poble Espanyol. Ⓜ Espanya.
Ⓦ laterrrazza.com.
Open-air summer club for
nonstop dance, house and techno.
Don't get there until 3am and
be prepared for the style police.
Entry charge.

Port Olímpic and Poblenou

The main waterfront legacy of the 1992 Olympics was the Port Olímpic, the marina development which lies fifteen minutes' walk along the promenade from Barceloneta. Locals make full use of the beach and boardwalks, descending in force at the weekends for a leisurely lunch or late drink in one of the scores of restaurants and bars. There are also fine beaches further north near the old working-class neighbourhood of Poblenou, while the impressive Museu Blau anchors the waterside zone known as the Parc del Fòrum. Access to the area is by metro to Ciutadella-Vila Olímpica or Poblenou, or bus #59 runs from La Rambla through Barceloneta and out to Port Olímpic.

Port Olímpic

MAP P.91, POCKET MAP K8–M8.
Ⓜ Ciutadella-Vila Olímpica.

As you approach the Olympic port, the golden mirage above the promenade slowly reveals itself to be a huge **copper fish** (courtesy of Frank Gehry, architect of the Bilbao Guggenheim). It's the emblem of the seafront development constructed for the 1992 Olympics, incorporating the port itself – site of many of the Olympic watersports events – which is backed by the city's two tallest buildings, the **Torre Mapfre** and the steel-framed **Hotel Arts Barcelona**, both 154m high. For many years the port has been home to a double-

Port Olímpic

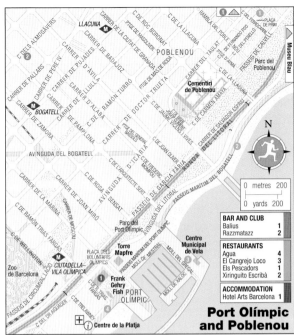

Port Olímpic and Poblenou

BAR AND CLUB
Balius	1
Razzmatazz	2

RESTAURANTS
Agua	4
El Cangrejo Loco	3
Els Pescadors	1
Xiringuito Escribà	2

ACCOMMODATION
Hotel Arts Barcelona	1

decker tier of raucous tourist bars and restaurants, but a complete redesign is underway, and it was hoped that by the time of the Americas Cup in 2024 these will have been replaced by high-end gastro temples and businesses focusing on sustainability and marine life.

City beaches

MAP P.91, POCKET MAP L8–M8.
From Ⓜ Ciutadella-Vila Olímpica it's a 15min walk along the promenade to Bogatell beach. Ⓦ bcn.cat/platges.
A series of sandy beaches stretches for four kilometres north of Port Olímpic. Split into different named sections (Nova Icària, Bogatell and so on), all of which have showers, playgrounds and open-air café-bars – pretty extraordinary facilities to find so close to a city centre. A sunny day, even in winter, brings the locals out in force, and the sands are regularly swept and replenished.

Centre de la Platja

MAP P.91, POCKET MAP K8.
Pg. Marítim. Ⓜ Ciutadella-Vila Olímpica.
Ⓦ bit.ly/CentrePlatja.
On the boardwalk arcade, in front of the Hospital del Mar, is a council-run beach visitor centre. There's a full programme of walks, talks and sports, as well as buckets and spades for kids, and volleyball and beach tennis gear available for pick-up games on the sands.

Rambla del Poblenou

MAP P.91.
Ⓜ Poblenou.
A twenty-minute walk up the beach from Port Olímpic, the Rambla de Poblenou runs through the most attractive part of **Poblenou** ("New Village"). The old industrial neighbourhood is at the heart of a huge city regeneration scheme, but the local avenue remains unchanged – a run of modest shops, cafés and restaurants,

Museu Blau

including the classic juice and milk bar of *El Tio Che* (Rambla de Poblenou 44–46).

Cementiri del Poblenou

MAP P.91, POCKET MAP M7.
Av. d'Icària. Ⓜ Bogatell.
This vast nineteenth-century mausoleum has its tombs set in walls 7m high. With birdsong accompanying a stroll around the flower-lined pavements, quiet courtyards and chapels, this village of the dead is a rare haven of peace in the city.

Museu Blau

MAP P.91, POCKET MAP M7.
Pl. Leonardo da Vinci 4–5, Parc del Fòrum. Ⓜ El Maresme Fòrum, or tram. Ⓦ museuciencies.bcn.cat. Charge, includes entrance to Jardí Botànic de Barcelona; free first Sun of the month and every Sun from 3pm.
The million-strong collection of rocks, fossils, plants and animals of the Museu de Ciències Naturals (Natural History Museum) has a state-of-the-art home in the visually stunning Blue Museum, housed in the Fòrum building, whose permanent exhibition – Planeta Vida (Planet Life) – plots a journey through the history of life on earth. It's heavily focused on evolutionary, whole-earth, Gaia principles, with plenty of entertaining, interactive bells and whistles to guide you through topics as diverse as sex and reproduction and conservation of the environment.

Diagonal Mar

The waterfront district north of Poblenou was developed in the wake of the Universal Forum of Cultures Expo (held in 2004). It's promoted as **Diagonal Mar**, anchored by the Diagonal Mar shopping mall (Ⓜ El Maresme Fòrum or tram T4) and with several classy hotels, convention centres and exhibition halls grouped nearby. The dazzling **Edifici Fòrum** building is the work of Jacques Herzog (architect of London's Tate Modern), while the main open space is claimed to be the second-largest square in the world after Beijing's Tiananmen Square. This immense expanse spreads towards the sea, culminating in a giant solar-panelled canopy that overlooks the marina, beach and park areas. In summer, temporary bars, dancefloors and chill-out zones are established at the **Parc del Fòrum**, and the city authorities have shifted some of the bigger annual music festivals and events down here to inject a bit of life outside convention time. At other times it can be a bit soulless, but it's definitely worth the metro or tram ride if you're interested in heroic-scale public projects.

Restaurants

Agua

MAP P.91, POCKET MAP K8.
Pg. Marítim 30. Ⓜ Ciutadella-Vila Olímpica.
Ⓦ somosesencia.es.

The nicest boardwalk restaurant on the strip, with a contemporary Mediterranean menu, from salads to grills, and tables along the beach. Prices are pretty fair, so it's usually busy. €€

El Cangrejo Loco

MAP P.91, POCKET MAP L8.
Moll de Gregal 29–30. Ⓜ Ciutadella-Vila Olímpica. Ⓦ elcangrejoloco.com.

The terrace at the "Crazy Crab" offers sea views, and the food is first rate. A mixed fried-fish plate is a typically Catalan starter, and the rice dishes are thoroughly recommended, including their paella. €€

Els Pescadors

MAP P.91, POCKET MAP M7.
Pl. Prim 1. Ⓜ Poblenou.
Ⓦ elspescadors.com.

The best fish restaurant in Barcelona? It's a tough call, but many would choose this hideaway place in a pretty Poblenou square. The menu offers daily fresh fish dishes, and plenty more involving rice, noodles or salted cod. Don't go mad, and you can eat here well for a reasonable price. €€€

Xiringuito Escribà

MAP P.91, POCKET MAP M8.
Ronda del Litoral 42, Platja Bogatell.
Ⓜ Ciutadella-Vila Olímpica.
Ⓦ xiringuitoescriba.com.

Beachfront restaurant (really a glorified beach shack) that's enough off the beaten track (a 15min walk from Port Olímpic) to mark you out as in the know. High points are paellas and daily fish specials, followed by sensational cakes and pastries from the Escribà family patisserie. €€€

Bar

Balius

MAP P.91, POCKET MAP M6.
C/de Pujades 196. Ⓜ Poblenou.
Ⓦ baliusbar.com.

The amount of drinking and eating options in Poblenou has not kept pace with the area's sudden popularity among young loft-dwelling types, and consequently *Balius* is rammed every night. Set in a converted pharmacy, it's a handsome space for cocktails and craft beer.

Club

Razzmatazz

MAP P.91, POCKET MAP L5.
C/Pamplona 88. Ⓜ Bogatell.
Ⓦ salarazzmatazz.com.

Razzmatazz hosts the biggest in-town rock gigs, and at weekends turns into "five clubs in one", spinning mixed sounds in variously named bars. Entry charge varies.

PORT OLÍMPIC AND POBLENOU

Gig at Razzmatazz

Dreta de l'Eixample

The nineteenth-century street grid north of Plaça de Catalunya is the city's main shopping and business district. It was designed as part of a revolutionary urban plan – the Eixample in Catalan ("Extension" or "Widening") – that divided districts into regular blocks, whose characteristic wide streets and shaved corners survive today. Two parallel avenues, Passeig de Gràcia and Rambla de Catalunya, are the backbone of the Eixample, with everything to the east of Rambla de Catalunya known as the Dreta de l'Eixample (the right-hand side). It's here that the bulk of the city's famous *modernista* (Catalan Art Nouveau) buildings are found, along with an array of classy galleries and some of the city's most stylish shops. Start your exploration from either Metro Passeig de Gràcia or Metro Diagonal.

Passeig de Gràcia

MAP P.96, POCKET MAP H1/4.
Ⓜ **Passeig de Gràcia.**

The prominent avenue, which runs northwest from Plaça de Catalunya, was laid out in its present form in 1827. It later developed as a showcase for

Passeig de Gràcia

modernista architects, eagerly commissioned by status-conscious merchants and businessmen. Walk the length of Passeig de Gràcia from Plaça de Catalunya to Avinguda Diagonal (a 25min stroll) and you'll pass some of the city's most extraordinary architecture, notably the famous group of buildings (including casas Amatller and Batlló) known as the Mansana de la Discòrdia, or "Block of Discord", as they show off wildly varying manifestations of the *modernista* style and spirit. Further up is Antoni Gaudí's iconic apartment building La Pedrera, while in between, wrought-iron Art Nouveau street lamps, fashion stores and designer hotels set the tone for this resolutely upscale avenue.

Museu del Perfum

MAP P.96, POCKET MAP H3.
Pg. de Gràcia 39. Ⓜ Passeig de Gràcia.
Ⓦ museodelperfume.com. Charge.
At the back of the Regia perfume store is a private collection of over five thousand perfume and essence bottles from Egyptian times

Casa Batlló

onwards. There are some exquisite pieces, including Turkish filigree-and-crystal ware and bronze and silver Indian elephant flasks, while more modern times are represented by scents made for Brigitte Bardot, Grace Kelly and Elizabeth Taylor.

Casa Amatller

MAP P.96, POCKET MAP G3.
Fundació Amatller, Pg. de Gràcia 41.
Ⓜ Passeig de Gràcia. Ⓦ amatller.org.
Charge.

Josep Puig i Cadafalch's striking Casa Amatller (1900) was designed for Antoni Amatller, a Catalan chocolate manufacturer, art collector, photographer and traveller. It's awash with coloured ceramic decoration, while inside the hallway twisted stone columns are interspersed with dragon lamps. Guided tours are occasionally available (check website for details) and usually include a visit to Amatller's photographic studio as well as chocolate tasting in the original kitchen. The house also displays temporary exhibitions under the auspices of the Amatller Institute of Hispanic Art.

Casa Batlló

MAP P.96, POCKET MAP G3.
Pg. de Gràcia 43. Ⓜ Passeig de Gràcia.
Ⓦ casabatllo.es. Charge.

The most extraordinary creation on the "Block of Discord" is the Casa Batlló, designed for the industrialist Josep Batlló and finished in 1907. Antoni Gaudí created an undulating facade that Salvador Dalí later compared to "the tranquil waters of a lake". The sinuous interior, meanwhile, resembles the inside of some great organism, complete with meandering, snakeskinpatterned walls. Self-guided audio tours show you the main floor, the patio and rear facade, the ribbed attic and celebrated mosaic rooftop chimneys. Advance tickets are recommended (by phone, in person or online); the scrum of visitors can be a frustrating business at peak times.

Fundació Antoni Tàpies

MAP P.96, POCKET MAP G3.
C/Aragó 255. Ⓜ Passeig de Gràcia.
Ⓦ fundaciotapies.org. Charge.

The definitive collection of the work of Catalan abstract artist

Dreta de l'Eixample

RESTAURANTS AND TAPAS BARS

2254	5
La Bodegueta	2
El Mussol	3, 10
El Nacional Barcelona	8
Tapas, 24	7
Tragaluz	1

CAFÉS

Café del Centre	6
Forn de Sant Jaume	4
Laie Llibreria Café	9

SHOPS

Bulevard dels Antiquaris	4
Casa del Llibro	3
Cubiñá	2
Mango	6
Purificación García	1
Reserva Ibérica	5

ACCOMMODATION

Casa Bonay	7
Hostal Girona	9
Hostal Goya	8
Hotel Condes de Barcelona	3
Mandarin Oriental	6
Praktik Bakery Hotel	2
Room-Mate Anna	4
Safestay Passeig de Gràcia	5
Sir Victor	1

Mercat Abaceria Central

Casa Fuster

GRÀCIA

Palau Robert

Casa Comalat

Palau Baró de Quadras

Casa de les Punxes

La Pedrera

Casa Thomas

Palau Montaner

Fundació Antoni Tàpies

Museu Egipci

La Concepció

Casa Batlló
Casa Amatller

Museu del Perfum

Mercat de la Concepció

Jardins de les Torres de les Aigües

Museu del Modernisme Català

GRAN VIA DE LES CORTS CATALANES

Casa Calvet

PLAÇA DE CATALUNYA

Palau de la Música Catalana

| 0 | metres | 200 |
| 0 | yards | 200 |

Antoni Tàpies i Puig (who died in 2012) is housed in *modernista* architect Lluís Domènech i Montaner's first important building, the Casa Montaner i Simon (1880). You can't miss it – the foundation building is capped by Tàpies's own striking sculpture, *Núvol i Cadira* ("Cloud and Chair", 1990), a tangle of glass, wire and aluminium. The artist was born in Barcelona in 1923 and was a founding member (1948) of the influential avant-garde Dau al Set ("Die at Seven") artists' group. Tàpies's abstract style matured in the 1950s, with underlying messages and themes signalled by the inclusion of everyday objects and symbols on the canvas. Changing exhibitions focus on selections of Tàpies's work, while other shows highlight works by various contemporary artists.

Museo Egipci de Barcelona

Museu Egipci de Barcelona

MAP P.96, POCKET MAP H3.
C/de València 284. Ⓜ Passeig de Gràcia.
Ⓦ museuegipci.com. Charge.

Barcelona's Egyptian Museum is an exceptional private collection of over a thousand ancient artefacts, from amulets to sarcophagi – there's nothing else in Spain quite like it. Visitors are given a detailed English-language guidebook, but the real pleasure is a serendipitous wander, turning up items like cat mummies or the rare figurine of a spoonbill (ibis) representing an Egyptian god. There are temporary exhibitions, plus a good shop and terrace café, while the museum also hosts children's activities and themed events.

Modernisme

The Catalan offshoot of Art Nouveau, **modernisme**, was the expression of a renewed upsurge in Catalan nationalism in the 1870s. Its most famous exponent was **Antoni Gaudí i Cornet** (1852–1926), whose buildings are apparently lunatic flights of fantasy, which at the same time are perfectly functional. His architectural influences were Moorish and Gothic, while he embellished his work with elements from the natural world. The imaginative impetus he provided inspired others like **Lluís Domènech i Montaner** (1850–1923) – perhaps the greatest *modernista* architect – and **Josep Puig i Cadafalch** (1867–1957), both of whom also experimented with the use of ceramic tiles, ironwork, stained glass and stone carving. This combination of traditional methods with modern technology became the hallmark of *modernisme* – producing some of the most exciting architecture to be found anywhere in the world.

Palau Montaner

Jardins de les Torres de les Aigües

MAP P.96, POCKET MAP H3.
C/Roger de Llúria 56, between C/Consell de Cent and C/Diputació. Ⓜ Girona. Free.

The original nineteenth-century Eixample urban plan – by utopian architect Ildefons Cerdà – was drawn up with local inhabitants very much in mind. Space, light and social community projects were part of the grand design, and something of the original municipal spirit can be seen in the Jardins de les Torres de les Aigües, an enclosed square (reached down a herringbone-brick tunnel) centred on a Moorish-style water tower. It has been handsomely restored by the city council, though the wide paddling pool has been allowed to dry up. Another example of the old Eixample lies directly opposite, across C/Roger de Llúria, where the cobbled **Passatge del Permanyer** cuts across an Eixample block, lined by candy-coloured, single-storey townhouses.

Mercat de la Concepció

MAP P.96, POCKET MAP J3.
Between C/de Valencia and C/d'Aragó.
Ⓜ Girona. Ⓦ laconcepcio.com.

Flowers, shrubs and plants are a Concepció speciality (the florists on Carrer de Valencia are open 24 hours a day), and there are some good snack bars inside the market and a few outdoor cafés to the side. The market takes its name from the nearby church of **La Concepció** (entrance on Carrer de Roger de Llúria), whose quiet cloister is a surprising haven of slender columns and orange trees.

Palau Montaner

MAP P.96, POCKET MAP H3.
C/de Mallorca 278. Ⓜ Passeig de Gràcia.
Ⓦ rutadelmodernisme.com. Guided visits, for groups only, reservations required. Charge.

The Palau Montaner (1896) has a curious history – after the original architect quit, Lluís Domènech i Montaner took over halfway through construction, and the top half of the facade is clearly more elaborate than the lower part. Meanwhile, the period's most celebrated craftsmen were set to work on the interior, which sports rich mosaic floors, painted glass, carved woodwork and a monumental staircase.

The building is now the seat of the Madrid government's delegation to Catalunya, but it is possible to arrange **guided tours** that explain something of the house's history and show you the lavish public rooms, grand dining room and courtyard. It's unusual to be able to get inside a private *modernista* house of the period, so it's definitely worth the effort.

La Pedrera

MAP P.96, POCKET MAP H2.
Pg. de Gràcia 92, entrance on C/Provença. Ⓜ Diagonal . Ⓦ lapedrera.com. Charge.

Antoni Gaudí's weird apartment building at the top of Passeig de Gràcia is simply not to be missed – though you can expect queues whenever you visit. Popularly known as La Pedrera, "the stone quarry", its rippled facade, curving around the street corner in one smooth sweep, is said to have been inspired by the mountain of Montserrat, while the apartments themselves resemble eroded cave dwellings. Indeed, there's not a straight line to be seen – hence the contemporary joke that the new tenants would only be able to keep snakes as pets. The self-guided visit includes a trip up to the extraordinary *terrat* (roof terrace) to see at close quarters the enigmatic chimneys – you should note that the roof terrace is often closed if it's raining. In addition, there's an excellent exhibition about Gaudí's life and work installed under the 270 curved brick arches of the attic. **El Pis** ("the apartment"), on the building's fourth floor, re-creates the design and style of a *modernista*-era bourgeois apartment in a series of extraordinarily light rooms that flow seamlessly from one to another. The apartment is filled with period furniture and effects, while the moulded door and window frames, and even the brass door handles, all follow Gaudí's sinuous building design. During the **Nits d'estiu** ("summer nights" – advance booking essential) you can enjoy the amazing rooftop by night with a complimentary glass of cava and music, while other concerts are also held at La Pedrera at various times.

Through the grand main entrance of the building there's access to the Pedrera **exhibition hall**, which hosts temporary art shows of works by major international artists.

Palau Robert

MAP P.96, POCKET MAP H2.
Pg. de Gràcia 107. Ⓜ Diagonal. Ⓦ gencat. cat/palaurobert. Free.

Visit the information centre for the Catalunya region for regularly changing exhibitions on all matters Catalan, from art to business. There are several exhibition spaces, both inside the main palace – built as a typical aristocratic residence in 1903 – and in the old coach house. The centre is also an important concert venue for recitals and orchestras, while the gardens around the back are a popular meeting point for local nannies and their charges.

La Pedrera

Palau Baró de Quadras

Palau Baró de Quadras

MAP P.96, POCKET MAP H2.
Av. Diagonal 373 Ⓜ Diagonal. Ⓦ llull.cat.
Free.

The beautifully detailed Palau
Baró de Quadras (a Josep Puig
i Cadafalch work from 1904)
now serves as the headquarters
of the Institut Ramon Llull,
an organization that promotes
Catalan language studies at
universities worldwide. Though
most of the building is closed
to the public, visitors can look
around its stunningly ornate
ground floor during the institute's
opening hours. If you first see
the building from the Avinguda
Diagonal side, be sure to walk
around to Carrer del Rosselló
– this side of the building is
decorated in a more subdued, but
very lovely, *modernista* style.

Casa de les Punxes

MAP P.96, POCKET MAP H2.
Av. Diagonal 416–420. Ⓜ Diagonal.
Ⓦ casalespunxes.com.
Cadafalch's largest work, the
soaring Casa Terrades, is more
usually known as the Casa de

les Punxes ("House of Spikes")
because of its red-tiled turrets and
steep gables. Built in 1903 for
three sisters, and converted from
three separate houses spreading
around an entire corner of a
block, the crenellated structure
is almost northern European in
style, reminiscent of a Gothic
castle.

Passatge Permanyer

MAP P.96, POCKET MAP H3.
Passatge Permanyer. Ⓜ Girona.
If this elegant, leafy alleyway cut
into one of the monolithic blocks
of the Eixample reminds you
of London, it's no coincidence.
Ildefons Cerdà, who planned this
part of the city's expansion, took
inspiration from Regent's Park
and included green spaces in the
centre of his squares. Most of
them were built over immediately
– if they were built at all – and
now contain car parks and retail
space, but 46 alleys (*passatges*),
of which Permanyer is the best
preserved, break up the urban grid
and lend a glimpse of what could
have been.

Shops

Bulevard dels Antiquaris

MAP P.96, POCKET MAP H3.
Pg. de Gràcia 55–57. Ⓜ Passeig de Gràcia.
Ⓦ bulevarddelsantiquaris.com.
An arcade with over seventy shops full of antiques – from toys and dolls to Spanish ceramics and African art.

Casa del Llibro

MAP P.96, POCKET MAP H3.
Pg. de Gràcia 62. Ⓜ Passeig de Gràcia.
Ⓦ casadellibro.com.
Barcelona's biggest book emporium with lots of English-language titles and Catalan literature in translation.

Cubiñà

MAP P.96, POCKET MAP H3.
C/Mallorca 291 Ⓜ Verdaguer
Ⓦ cubinya.es.
The building is stupendous – Domènech i Montaner's *modernista* Casa Thomas – while inside holds the very latest in household design.

Mango

MAP P.96, POCKET MAP H4.
Pg. de Gràcia 36, plus others. Ⓜ Passeig de Gràcia. Ⓦ mango.com.
Barcelona is where high-street fashion chain Mango began. For last season's gear at unbeatable prices, head to Mango Outlet (Carrer de Girona 37).

Purificación García

MAP P.96, POCKET MAP H2.
C/de Provença 292. Ⓜ Diagonal.
Ⓦ purificaciongarcia.es.
A hot designer with an eye for fabrics – García's first job was in a textile factory. She's also designed clothes for film and theatre, and her costumes were seen at the opening ceremony of the Barcelona Olympics.

Reserva Ibérica

MAP P.96, POCKET MAP G3.

Rambla de Catalunya 61. Ⓜ Passeig de Gràcia. Ⓦ reservaiberica.com.
A ham wonderland specializing in *jamón ibérico de bellota*, the finest of all the Spanish cured hams, which comes from acorn-fed pigs. Pick up pre-packaged samplers or tuck into a plate of paper-thin slices at one of the marble-topped tables.

Cafés

Cafè del Centre

MAP P.96, POCKET MAP J3.
C/Girona 69. Ⓜ Girona.
Ⓦ cafedelcentre.com.
This beautiful old bar has been here since 1873 (a plaque outside honours its service to the city) and, despite new ownership and a complete overhaul, it has retained many of its *modernista* features. Not as sleepy as it once was, it now attracts a younger, more energetic crowd at night. €

Mango outlet store in Parc Valles de Terrassa shopping centre

Forn de Sant Jaume

MAP P.96, POCKET MAP G3.
Rambla de Catalunya 50.
Ⓜ Passeig de Gràcia.
Ⓦ instagram.com/forndesantjaume.
Uptown *pastisseria* whose glittering
windows are piled high with
croissants, cakes, pastries and
sweets. The small adjacent café has
rambla seats, or you can take away
your goodies for later. €

Laie Llibreria Café

MAP P.96, POCKET MAP H4.
C/Pau Claris 85. Ⓜ Passeig de Gràcia.
Ⓦ laie.es.
The city's first and best bookshop-
café (buy a book downstairs and
take it to the café to read) is known
for its popular weekday buffet
breakfast spread, set lunch deals
and à la carte dining. €

Restaurants and tapas bars

2254

MAP P.96, POCKET MAP G3.

C/del Consell de Cent 335.
Ⓜ Passeig de Gràcia.
Ⓦ 2254restaurant.com.
The name of the restaurant stands
for the number of kilometres
between Barcelona and Palermo
– the birthplace of the restaurant
owner and chef, Nuncio Cona.
Creative, tasty dishes with not only
Spanish influences, but also Italian,
French and from further afield. Try
the gyoza stuffed with oxtail or the
lamb shank with mustard, mint
and yoghurt. €€€

La Bodegueta

MAP P.96, POCKET MAP G2.
Rambla Catalunya 100. Ⓜ Diagonal.
Ⓦ labodeguetarambla.com.
This long-established *bodega* offers
cava and wine by the glass, as well
as ham, cheese, anchovies and other
tapas to soak it up. €€

El Mussol

MAP P.96, POCKET MAP G3, E10.
C/Aragó 261 Ⓜ Passeig de Gràcia
Ⓦ mussolrestaurant.com.
Chain of big rustic diners, known
for their meat and vegetables *a*

El Nacional Barcelona

Patatas bravas

la brasa – from the grill. They're good places to sample hearty Catalan country cooking, with snails and wild mushrooms on the menu all year round and *calçots* (big spring onions) a spring speciality. There's another branch at Carrer de Casp 19. €

El Nacional Barcelona

MAP P.96, POCKET MAP H4.
Pg. de Gràcia 24 Bis. Ⓜ **Passeig de Gràcia.**
Ⓦ **elnacionalbcn.com.**
A massive one-stop-shop for Spanish cuisine; in this gorgeous, high-ceilinged space you'll find a fish restaurant, grill, tapas bar, snack bar, oyster bar, wine bar, cocktail bar and most other bars you can think of. Check it out on the cheap with a quick snack or go for broke with a massive extra-aged rib-eye steak from the wood grill. €€€

Tapas, 24

MAP P.96, POCKET MAP H4.
C/Diputació 269. Ⓜ **Passeig de Gràcia.**
Ⓦ **carlesabellan.com.**
Star chef Carles Abellan gets back to his roots at this basement tapas bar. There's a reassuringly traditional feel that's echoed in the menu, which features *patatas bravas*, Andalucian-style fried fish, meatballs, chorizo sausage and fried eggs, as well as sharing plates. But the kitchen updates the classics too, so there's also *calamares romana* (fried squid) dyed black with squid ink or a burger with foie gras. There's always a rush and a bustle at meal times, so be aware you might have to queue. €€

Tragaluz

MAP P.96, POCKET MAP G2.
Ptge. de la Concepció 5. Ⓜ **Diagonal.**
Ⓦ **grupotragaluz.com.**
A stylish uptown standby that attracts beautiful people by the score, and the classy Mediterranean-with-knobs-on cooking, served under a glass roof (*tragaluz* means "skylight"), doesn't disappoint. The menu ranges from varied pasta dishes to grilled sea bass, and it's a relaxing stop for those fresh off the *modernista* trail (La Pedrera is just across the way). €€€

Sagrada Família and Glòries

If there's one building that is an essential stop on any visit to Barcelona, it's Antoni Gaudí's great church of the Sagrada Família (Metro Sagrada Família). Most visitors make a special journey out to see it and then head back into the centre, but it's worth sticking around to visit Lluís Domènech i Montaner's *modernista* hospital (now known as the Recinte Modernista de Sant Pau). A few blocks south of Sagrada Família you'll find the Glòries area and a further set of attractions, including the city's main concert hall and music museum, and Catalunya's flagship national theatre building.

Sagrada Família

MAP P.106, POCKET MAP K2.
C/Mallorca 401. Ⓜ Sagrada Família.
Ⓦ sagradafamilia.org. Charge, combination ticket with Casa-Museu Gaudí available.

The metro drops you right outside the overpowering church of the Sagrada Família ("Sacred Family"). Begun in 1882 on a modest scale, the project changed the minute that 31-year-old architect Antoni Gaudí took charge in 1884 – he saw in the Sagrada Família an opportunity to reflect his own deepening spiritual feelings. Gaudí spent the rest of his life working on the church and was adapting the plans right up to his untimely death. Run over by a tram on June 7, 1926, his death was treated as a Catalan national disaster, and all of Barcelona turned out for his funeral.

Although the building survived, Gaudí's plans were mostly destroyed during the Spanish Civil War. Nevertheless, work restarted in the 1950s

Sagrada Família

Recinte Modernista de Sant Pau

amid great controversy, and has continued ever since – as have the arguments. Some maintained that the Sagrada Família should be left incomplete as a memorial to Gaudí, others that the architect intended it to be the work of several generations. Either way, based on reconstructed models and notes, the project is now moving towards completion (in 2026, it is said), and the building is beginning to take its final shape.

The size alone is startling (Gaudí's original plan was to build a church to seat over 10,000 people), while the carved spires, monumental bronze doors and vibrant facades are an imaginative and symbolic *tour de force*. Gaudí made extensive use of human, plant and animal models to exactly produce the likenesses he sought – the spreading stone leaves of the roof in the church interior, for example, were inspired by the city's plane trees. A **lift** up one of the towers provides an unforgettable close-up view of the work, while in the **crypt** (where Gaudí is buried) a fascinating museum traces the construction of the church – you can also view sculptors and model-makers still at work today.

Recinte Modernista de Sant Pau

MAP P.106, POCKET MAP M1.
C/de Sant Antoni Maria Claret 167. Ⓜ Sant Pau Dos de Maig. Ⓦ santpaubarcelona.org. **Charge.**

Lluís Domènech i Montaner's *modernista* public hospital is possibly the one building that can touch the Sagrada Família for size and invention. It's hard to believe that its whimsical pavilions and towers, which are adorned with sculpture, mosaics, stained glass and ironwork, were once a working hospital, but it remained fully functional until 2009. A massive clean-up project has restored the historical complex's glory, while the business of curing the sick has moved to an ugly modern complex next door. The original building is now home to health and sustainability NGOs, not recovering patients. Interesting tours of the old hospital run regularly and the breathtaking central courtyard

ACCOMMODATION	
Urbany Hostel Barcelona	1
Hotel Eurostars Monumental	2

RESTAURANTS AND TAPAS BARS	
Bardeni - el Meatbar	5
Casa Rafols	8
Firo Tast	1
Parking Pizza	7
Puertecillo Sagrada Família	3
La Taquería	4

CAFÉS	
Granja Petitbo	6
Puiggrós	2

SHOPS	
Centre Comercial Barcelona Glòries	1
Els Encants Vells	2

BAR	
JazzMan	1

—T4— Tram

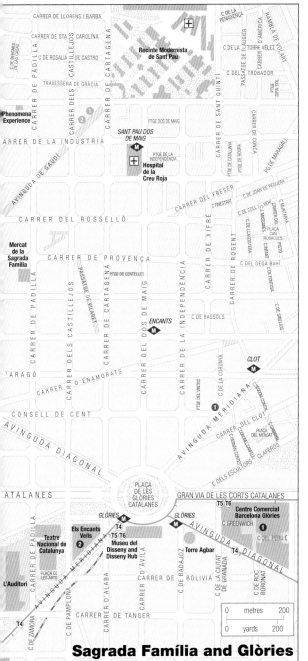

Sagrada Família and Glòries

Casa Macaya

is a popular venue for outdoor concerts and fashion shows. It's an easy stroll up here from the Sagrada Família.

Casa Macaya

MAP P.106, POCKET MAP J2.
Pg. de Sant Joan 108. Ⓜ Verdaguer.
Just four blocks from the Sagrada Família, Josep Puig i Cadafalch's Casa Macaya (1898–1900) is well known for its imaginative exterior carvings by craftsman Eusebi Arnau – look for the angel holding a camera or the sculptor himself on his way to work by bike.

Plaça de les Glòries Catalanes

MAP P.106, POCKET MAP M4.
Ⓜ Glòries.
Barcelona's major avenues all meet at Plaça de les Glòries Catalanes, dedicated to the Catalan "glories", from architecture to literature. Glòries is at the centre of the city's latest bout of regeneration. Signature buildings are Jean Nouvel's cigar-shaped **Torre Glòries**, a remarkable aluminium-and-glass tower inspired by

Montserrat, and the sleek, zinc-plated Museu del Disseny (Design Museum). Nearby **Parc del Clot** shows what can be done in an urban setting within the remains of a razed factory site. Trams speed down Avinguda Diagonal to the Diagonal Mar district, passing the **Parc del Centre del Poblenou** (10min walk, or tram stop Pere IV), another park on an old industrial site.

Casa Planells

MAP P.106, POCKET MAP K3.
Av. Diagonal 332. Ⓜ Verdaguer.
This 1924 residential building by lesser-known *modernista* architect Josep Maria Jujol is understated and austere by the standards of his contemporaries, but still features organic, flowing lines. Jujol was given a free hand to do whatever he wanted with the small space available and came up with an anachronistic design that remains unique. Its interior is closed to the public but the exterior oval windows and intricate cast-iron railings are worth seeing.

Església de les Saleses

MAP P.106, POCKET MAP K3.
Passeig de Sant Joan 86–92. Ⓜ Tetuan.
Ⓦ parroquiaconcepciobcn.org. Free.
This fine neo-Gothic church and former convent – and later, monastery – was designed by Joan Martorell i Montells. His student, one Antoni Gaudí, may also have worked on it during its construction, which was between 1882 and 1885. The beginnings of Catalan *modernisme* can be seen in the church's ornate details, but it suffered damage during the Setmana Trágica (Tragic Week) of 1909. It was also set alight in 1936 during the Spanish Civil War, when the bodies of nuns were pulled from its crypts and gruesomely displayed on the street. Today, the church has been extensively restored and the monastery is now a school.

Museu del Disseny

MAP P.106, POCKET MAP M4.
Pl. de les Glòries Catalanes 37–38.
Ⓜ Glòries. Ⓦ barcelona.cat/
museudelldisseny. Charge.

The new Museu del Disseny brings together Barcelona's applied art collections inside the Disseny Hub building. In addition to the museum, the Hub is also home to temporary exhibition spaces, a public library and the headquarters of local design institutions such as the Foment de les Arts i del Disseny (FAD).

Teatre Nacional de Catalunya

MAP P.106, POCKET MAP L4/5.
Pl. de les Arts 1. Ⓜ Glòries. Ⓦ tnc.cat.

Catalunya's National Theatre features an enterprising programme of classics, original works and productions by guest companies. The building itself makes a dramatic statement, presenting a soaring glass box encased within a Greek temple, and there are guided **tours** for anyone interested in learning more (Wed & Thurs, reservations required).

L'Auditori

MAP P.106, POCKET MAP L5.
C/Lepant 150. Ⓜ Glòries. Ⓦ auditori.cat.
Museu de la Música C/de Padilla 155.
Ⓦ bit.ly/MuseuMusica. Charge, free first Sun of the month, every Sun from 3pm and every Thurs from 6pm.

The city's main contemporary concert hall is home to the Barcelona Symphony Orchestra (OBC), though the programme includes chamber, choral, jazz and world concerts too. There's also the entertaining Museu de la Música (Music Museum), which displays a remarkable collection of historic instruments and musical devices.

Phenomena Experience

MAP P.106, POCKET MAP L1.
C/Sant Antoni Maria Claret 168.
Ⓜ Sant Pau Dos de Maig. Ⓦ phenomena-experience.com.

Fall in love again with the great movies of the seventies, eighties and nineties, plus selected recent blockbusters (all in their original language), at this independent cinema. The seats are comfortable, the screen is wide and the sound is state-of-the-art.

Museu del Disseny and Torre Agbar

Shops

Centre Comercial Barcelona Glòries
MAP P.106, POCKET MAP M4.
Av. Diagonal 208. Ⓜ Glòries.
Ⓦ lesglories.com.
Anchoring the neighbourhood is this huge mall with all the national high-street fashion names represented (H&M, Zara, Bershka, Mango) as well as a big Carrefour supermarket and an eight-screen cinema complex.

Els Encants Vells
MAP P.106, POCKET MAP L4.
Av. Meridiana 69. Ⓜ Glòries.
Ⓦ encantsbcn.com.
The city's flea market has a shiny home next to the Teatre Nacional de Catalunya. The site sports multiple levels of open-air treasure-hunting – you name it, you can buy it – all protected by a large canopy whose metallic underside reflects the bustling market below. You can also find surprisingly good food in the top-floor snack bars.

Els Encants Vells

Cafés

Granja Petitbo
MAP P.106, POCKET MAP J3.
Passeig de Sant Joan 82. Ⓜ Tetuan.
Ⓦ granjapetitbo.com.
The long, tree-lined Passeig de Sant Joan is now a hub of cool cafés and restaurants, but *Granja Petitbo* was one of the first to herald a turnaround in the fortunes of this neighbourhood – a friendly, shabby-chic place for coffee, brunch or lunch, with a handful of tables outside. €

Puiggròs
MAP P.106, POCKET MAP L1.
Av. Gaudí 77. Ⓜ Sant Pau Dos de Maig.
☎ 934 362 304.
Open since 1922, this family bakery has recently been stylishly renovated. Take your pick from tempting pastries, fresh bread and excellent coffee, then grab a seat on the terrace or inside to watch the bakers in their glass-walled workshop. €

Restaurants and tapas bars

Bardeni – el Meatbar
MAP P.106, POCKET MAP L3.
C/València 454. Ⓜ Sagrada Família.
Ⓦ bardeni.es.
Former Catalan chef of the year Dani Lechuga (whose surname ironically means "lettuce") is from a family of butchers and meat experts, so *Bardeni*'s raw materials are first rate. Beefy tapas like oxtail cannelloni and tacos are served, plus a few refined specials. €€

Casa Rafols
MAP P.106, POCKET MAP G11.
Ronda de Sant Pere 74. Ⓜ Arc de Triomf.
Ⓦ casarafols.com.
For over a century, *Rafols* was a celebrated *ferreteria* (ironmonger's) and still has the

Centre Comercial Barcelona Glòries

elaborate wrought-iron facade to show it. These days it's a slick combination of Art Deco cocktail bar and lively restaurant serving Mediterranean dishes in a high-ceilinged space or at tables outside on the pavement. €€€

Firo Tast

MAP P.106, POCKET MAP L1.
Av. Gaudí 83.  Sant Pau Dos de Maig. grupfiro.com.

Three *Firo* food businesses cluster together here and form a bright spot in a street full of mediocre tourist restaurants. The superb Chocofiro chocolatiers is flanked by *El Petit Firo* (a quality tapas bar) and *Firo Tast*, a sit-down restaurant serving a solid set menu of Catalan classics. €€

Parking Pizza

MAP P.106, POCKET MAP J4.
Passeig de Sant Joan 56. Tetuan. parkingpizza.com.

Housed in a former garage (hence the name) this is a vast operation, packed every night, with long communal tables and elbow-to-elbow dining. The pizzas, though,

are truly excellent, as are the starters and salads – the red quinoa with avocado and a poached egg is a favourite. €

La Taquería

MAP P.106, POCKET MAP K3.
Ptge. del Font 5. Sagrada Família. lataqueria.eu.

When it comes to Mexican food in Europe, throwing the word "authentic" around can get you in trouble with the purists, but it's an apt description for the menu here, which ranges from *tacos al pastor* to freshly made guacamole. €

Bar

JazzMan

MAP P.106, POCKET MAP K2.
C/Roger de Flor 238. Sagrada Família. jazzmanbarcelona.blogspot.com.

Everything you'd want from a cosy jazz club: low lights, live music, good drinks and a cool, intimate vibe. When there's no one on stage, expect to hear classics from *JazzMan's* impeccable vinyl and CD collection.

Esquerra de l'Eixample

The long streets west of Rambla de Catalunya as far as Barcelona Sants station are perhaps the least visited on any city sightseeing trip. With all the major architectural highlights found on the Eixample's eastern (or right-hand) side, the Esquerra de l'Eixample (left-hand side) was intended by its nineteenth-century planners for public buildings and institutions, many of which still stand. However, the Esquerra does have its moments of interest – not least a couple of excellent museums and an eye-catching public park or two – while it's here that some of the city's best bars and clubs are found, particularly in the gay-friendly streets of the so-called Gaixample district, near the university.

Universitat de Barcelona

MAP P.114, POCKET MAP F4–G4.
Gran Via de les Corts Catalanes 585, at Pl. de la Universitat. Ⓜ Universitat.

Built in the 1860s, the grand Neoclassical university building is now largely used for ceremonies and administration purposes, but you can visit the main hall or the fine arcaded courtyards and extensive gardens. The traditional student meeting point is the *Bar Estudantil*, outside in Plaça Universitat, where you can usually grab a pavement table.

Museu del Modernisme Català

MAP P.114, POCKET MAP G3.
C/Balmes 48. Ⓜ Passeig de Gràcia.
Ⓦ mmcat.cat. Charge.

Barcelona's traditional "gallery district", around Carrer del Consell de Cent, is a fitting

Universitat de Barcelona

location for the stupendous *modernista* collection housed in the Museu del Modernisme Català. It's the private enterprise of the celebrated Gothsland antiques gallery, and displays a collection forty years in the making – including the famous marble decorative vase by craftsman Eusebi Arnau that was the gallery's symbol for over thirty years. This is just one of 350 works on show across two exhibition floors in a restored former textile warehouse – the grand, vaulted basement contains paintings and sculpture while on the ground floor is Modernista furniture, from screens to sofas. There are paintings and works by many famous names, from oils by Ramon Casas i Carbó to sinuous mirrors and tables by Antoni Gaudí (originally made for the casas Batlló and Calvet). But above all, this is a rare opportunity to examine extraordinary Art Nouveau fixtures and fittings by less familiar artists: wonderful creations by pioneering cabinetmaker Joan Busquets i Jané, for example; the dramatic carved headboards of Gaspar Homar i Mezquida; or the expressive terracotta sculptures of Lambert Escaler i Milà. As a crash course in the varied facets of Catalan *modernisme*, beyond the iconic buildings themselves, it's invaluable.

Museu del Modernisme Català

Mercat del Ninot

MAP P.114, POCKET MAP F2/3.
C/Mallorca 133. Ⓜ Hospital Clínic.
Ⓦ mercatdelninot.com.

One of the oldest markets in the city has recently undergone a major refurbishment. The "new" Ninot is a treat for hungry shoppers, full of stallholders selling ready-to-eat dishes as well as fresh produce. The restaurant at the rear, *El Ninot Cuina*, is an understated gem. Around the back of the hospital, it's also worth having a look at the

Escola Industrial, formerly a textile mill, which boasts a 1920s chapel by Joan Rubió i Bellvér, who worked with Antoni Gaudí. Students usually fill the courtyards, and you're free to take a stroll through to view the highly decorative buildings.

Casa Golferichs

MAP P.114, POCKET MAP E4.
Gran Via de les Corts Catalanes 491.
Ⓜ Rocafort. Ⓦ golferichs.org.

In 1900, when road engineer and wood trader Macari Golferichs wanted to show off his success with a *modernista* mansion in the Eixample, he turned to the young architect Joan Rubió i Bellvor, one of Antoni Gaudí's closest collaborators. The result, known as El Xalet ("The Chalet") was a Gothic-tinged oddity, full of dark wood, ornate ceramics and soaring vertical lines. It is now a venue for intimate concerts, presentations and exhibitions.

municipal slaughterhouse. It features a raised piazza whose only feature is Joan Miró's gigantic mosaic sculpture *Dona i Ocell* ("Woman and Bird"), towering above a shallow reflecting pool. The rear of the park is given over to games areas and landscaped sections of palms and firs, with a kiosk café and some outdoor tables among the trees. The children's playground here is one of the best in the city.

Arenas de Barcelona

Parc Joan Miró

MAP P.114, POCKET MAP C3/4–D3/4.
C/de Tarragona. Ⓜ Tarragona.
Parc Joan Miró was laid out on the site of the nineteenth-century

Arenas de Barcelona

MAP P.114, POCKET MAP C4.
Gran Via de les Corts Catalanes
373–385, at Pl. d'Espanya. Ⓜ Espanya.
Ⓦ arenasdebarcelona.com.
The landmark building on the north side of Plaça d'Espanya is the fabulous Moorish-style bullring, the Arenas de Barcelona, originally built in 1900 but reimagined as a swish shopping and leisure centre that opened in 2011. On top is a

Esquerra de l'Eixample

ACCOMMODATION
Alternative Creative Youth Home	5
Midmost Hotel Barcelona	6
Nobu Hotel	1
Hotel Praktik Rambla	3
Hotel Soho	4
Somnio Barcelona	2

RESTAURANTS AND TAPAS BARS
Cerveseria Catalana	4
Cinc Sentits	8
Compartir	5
Disfrutar	2
La Flauta	7
Gresca	3
Manteca	6
La Taverna del Clínic	1

BARS
Aire Chicas	9
BierCaB	8
Dry Martini	4
Garage Beer Co.	7
Punto BCN	6
Quilombo	3
Velódromo	2

CLUBS
Antilla BCN	
Latin Club	5
City Hall	10
Luz de Gas	1

SHOPS
Altaïr	4
Antonio Miró	3
Estanc Duaso	2
Jean-Pierre Bua	1

On the Miró trail

When you've seen one Miró – well, you start to see them everywhere in Barcelona, starting with the large ceramic mural visible on the facade at the airport. The towering *Dona i Ocell* in the Parc Joan Miró is unmissable, but you should also look down at your feet on La Rambla for the pavement mural at Plaça de la Boqueria. Miró also designed the *Caixa de Pensions* starfish logo splashed across the CaixaForum arts centre. In many ways, it's a Miró city, whatever Picasso fans might think.

walkaround promenade circling the **dome** that offers 360-degree views, while inside are four floors of shopping and entertainment, including cinema, gym and various restaurants.

Parc de l'Espanya Industrial

MAP P.114, POCKET MAP B2/3–C2/3.
C/de Sant Antoni. Ⓜ Sants Estació.
If you have time to kill at Barcelona Sants station, nip around the south side to

Basque architect Luis Peña Ganchegui's urban park. Built on the site of an old textile factory, there's a line of concrete lighthouses contrasting with an incongruously classical Neptune, as well as a boating lake, café kiosk, playground and sports facilities. It's a decent attempt at reconciling local interests with the otherwise mundane nature of the surroundings, typical of the city's approach to revitalizing unkempt urban corners.

Shops

Altaïr

MAP P.114, POCKET MAP G4.
Gran Via de les Corts Catalanes 616.
Ⓜ Passeig de Gràcia. Ⓦ altair.es.
Europe's biggest travel superstore
has a massive selection of travel
books, guides, maps and world
music, plus a programme of travel-
related talks and exhibitions.

Antonio Miró

MAP P.114, POCKET MAP G3.
Enric Granados 46. Ⓜ Diagonal.
Ⓦ antoniomiro.com.
The showcase for Barcelona's most
innovative designer, now also
branding accessories and household
design items.

Estanc Duaso

MAP P.114, POCKET MAP G2.
C/Balmes 116. Ⓜ Diagonal/FGC Provença.
Ⓦ duaso.com.
Arnold Schwarzenegger shops for
his stogies in this cigar-smokers'
paradise that features a walk-
in humidor, in-store rolling
demonstrations and expert advice.

Jean Pierre Bua

MAP P.114, POCKET MAP F1.

Jean Pierre Bua clothing store

Av. Diagonal 469. Ⓜ Hospital Clínic.
Ⓦ jeanpierrebua.com.
The city's high temple for fashion: a
postmodern shrine for Yamamoto,
Gaultier, Miyake, Galliano,
McQueen, McCartney, Westwood
and other international stars.

Restaurants and tapas bars

Cerveseria Catalana

MAP P.114, POCKET MAP G3.
C/Mallorca 236. Ⓜ Passeig de Gràcia.
Ⓦ cerveceriacatalana.com.
A place that is serious about its
tapas and beer – the counters are
piled high, supplemented by a
blackboard list of daily specials,
while the walls are lined with
bottled brews from around the
world. It gets busy after work and
at meal times, and you might have
to wait for a table. €

Cinc Sentits

MAP P.114, POCKET MAP F3.
C/Entença 60. Ⓜ Universitat.
Ⓦ cincsentits.com.
Jordi Artal's "Five Senses" wows
diners with its contemporary
Catalan cuisine – and it has a

Disfrutar

Michelin star to boot, so you'll need to book. Two tasting menus (wine pairings available) use rigorously sourced ingredients (wild fish, mountain lamb, seasonal vegetables, farmhouse cheeses) in elegant, pared-down dishes that are all about flavour. €€€€

Compartir

MAP P.114, POCKET MAP G3.
C/ de València 225. Ⓜ Passeig de Gràcia. Ⓦ compartirbarcelona.com.
The more affordable little sister of the divine *Disfrutar* has the same culinary geniuses behind it and a similar approach to creative and stunning dishes (the pickled sardine dish with purple carrots, particularly, is a work of art).
The bold and eclectic decor, and unfussy service, make this a more informal experience than is usually paired with this level of cooking. €€€

Disfrutar

MAP P.114, POCKET MAP F2.
C/ de Villarroel 163. Ⓜ Hospital Clínic. Ⓦ disfrutarbarcelona.com.
A recipe for the hottest ticket in town: take three head chefs from

the former "world's best restaurant" *El Bulli*, add a labyrinthine Barcelona location, season with the smiles of happy customers and decorate with an instant Michelin star. The *Disfrutar* Festival tasting menu gets you 28 courses of magical creations and a lot of lasting memories. €€€€

La Flauta

MAP P.114, POCKET MAP F4.
C/Aribau 23. Ⓜ Universitat. ☎ 933 237 038.
One of the city's best-value lunch menus sees diners queuing for tables early – get there before 2pm to avoid the rush. While the name is a nod to the house speciality gourmet sandwiches (a *flauta* is a crispy baguette) there are also tapas-style meals served day and night. €

Gresca

MAP P.114, POCKET MAP G2.
C/Provença 230. Ⓜ Diagonal. Ⓦ gresca.rest.
Local food writers have unsuccessfully campaigned for years for chef Rafa Penya to have a Michelin star. But what's bad news for him is good news for diners: you get to keep eating his superb food

at bargain prices. The lunchtime menu is a winner, as is the offshoot tapas bar to one side. €€€

Manteca

MAP P.114, POCKET MAP D3.
C/Aribau 23. Ⓜ Rocafort.
Ⓦ bit.ly/MantecaB.

A welcome addition to a quiet corner of the Eixample, with tables outside on the newly pedestrianised Carrer de Consell de Cent. Sharing plates range from *patatas bravas* and chicken goujons to roast aubergine with citrus tahini, tomato and honey, and the atmosphere is cheerfully relaxed. €€

La Taverna del Clínic

MAP P.114, POCKET MAP F2.
C/Rosselló 155. Ⓜ Hospital Clínic.
Ⓦ latavernadelclinic.com.

Named for the hospital over the road, this is a gourmet tapas spot that concentrates on regional produce. Snack at the solid marble bar or sit down for serious food, accompanied by artisan olive oil and a high-class wine list, at one of the ten tables (book in advance). Quality is high but the bill runs up quickly, with dishes from crispy suckling pig to sea urchins artfully arranged on mounds of sea salt. €€€

La Taverna del Clínic

Bars

Aire Chicas

MAP P.114, POCKET MAP G3.
C/de Diputació 233. Ⓜ Passeig de Gràcia.
Ⓦ arenadisco.com.

The hottest, most stylish lesbian bar in town is a relaxed place for a drink and a dance to pop, house and retro sounds. Gay men are welcome too.

BierCaB

MAP P.114, POCKET MAP F3.
C/Muntaner 55. Ⓜ Universitat.
Ⓦ biercab.com.

Thirty international craft beers on tap, constantly updated via large screens, means that there's an ale to slake all thirsts here. The staff are enthusiastic and well-informed, and you can try before you buy. Prices, like most craft beer bars in Barcelona, are steep, so save some euros to pick up a bottle of your favourite from the adjoining shop.

Dry Martini

MAP P.114, POCKET MAP F2.
C/Aribau 166. Ⓜ Provença.
Ⓦ drymartiniorg.com.

White-jacketed bartenders, dark wood and brass fittings, a self-satisfied air – it could only be Barcelona's legendary uptown cocktail bar. To be fair though, no one in town mixes drinks better.

Garage Beer Co.

MAP P.114, POCKET MAP F3.
C/Consell de Cent 261. Ⓜ Universitat.
Ⓦ garagebeer.co.

This friendly brewpub was an early fixture on Barcelona's "beer mile" – the craft beer bar-filled area that's boomed in recent years. There are no frills, just great ales, simple snacks, wooden benches and a glass wall onto the microbrewery out back.

Punto BCN

MAP P.114, POCKET MAP F3.
C/Muntaner 63–65. Ⓜ Universitat.
Ⓦ arenadisco.com.

Gaixample classic that attracts a lively crowd for drinks, chat and music. Wednesday happy hour is a blast, while Friday night is party night.

Quilombo

MAP P.114, POCKET MAP F2.
C/Aribau 149. Ⓜ Provença.
Ⓦ quilombo.com.

Unpretentious music bar that's rolled with the years since 1971, featuring live guitarists, Latin American bands and a clientele that joins in enthusiastically, maracas in hand.

Velódromo

MAP P.114, POCKET MAP F1.
C/Muntaner 213. Ⓜ Hospital Clínic.
Ⓦ barvelodromo.com.

A gleaming facelift has put the glam back into this lofty, Parisian-style Art Deco gem. It's ideal for swish drinks and cocktails, though with an excellent breakfast, tapas and bistro menu, it's also made for early starts and later dinners.

Clubs

Antilla BCN Latin Club

MAP P.114, POCKET MAP E3.
C/Aragó 141–143. Ⓜ Urgell.
Ⓦ antillasalsa.com.

Latin and Caribbean tunes galore

Dry Martini

– rumba, son, salsa, merengue, mambo, you name it – for out-and-out good-time dancing. There are live bands, killer cocktails and dance classes most nights.

City Hall

MAP P.114, POCKET MAP G4.
Rambla de Catalunya 2–4. Ⓜ Plaça de Catalunya. Ⓦ cityhallbarcelona.com.

This medium-sized club, just off the Plaça Catalunya, thrums to techno and electronica most nights of the week, attracting a decent roster of local and international DJs. Earlier in the evening there are live flamenco shows (Ⓦ flamencobarcelonacity.com).

Luz de Gas

MAP P.114, POCKET MAP F1.
C/Muntaner 246. Ⓜ Provença.
Ⓦ luzdegas.com.

Smart live-music venue, housed in a former ballroom, which is popular with a slightly older crowd and hosts live bands (rock, blues, soul, jazz and covers) every night around midnight. Foreign acts appear regularly too, mainly jazz-blues types but also old soul acts and up-and-coming rockers. Entry charge varies.

Gràcia and Parc Güell

Gràcia was a village for much of its early existence, before being annexed as a suburb in the late nineteenth century. It still feels set apart from the city in many ways, and though actual sights are few and far between, it's well known for its cinemas, bars and restaurants. The one unmissable attraction, meanwhile, just on the neighbourhood fringe, is nearby Park Güell, an extraordinary flight of fancy by architectural genius Antoni Gaudí. To get to Gràcia take the FGC train from Plaça de Catalunya to Gràcia station, or the metro to either Diagonal (south) or Fontana (north). From any of the stations, it's around a 500m walk to Gràcia's main square, Plaça del Sol, hub of the neighbourhood's renowned nightlife.

Mercat de la Llibertat

MAP P.121, POCKET MAP G1.
Pl. Llibertat 27. Ⓜ Fontana.
Ⓦ mercatllibertat.cat.
You may as well start where the locals start first thing in the morning, shopping for bread and provisions in the neighbourhood market. The red-brick and iron structure has been beautifully restored and at *La Clau* you can join the locals for breakfast and a morning sharpener of wine or beer.

Casa Vicens

Casa Vicens

MAP P.121, POCKET MAP G1.
C/de les Carolines 24. Ⓜ Fontana.
Ⓦ casavicens.org. Charge.

Antoni Gaudí's first major private commission (1883–85) took its inspiration from the Moorish style, covering the facade of the house in green and white tiles with a flower motif. The decorative iron railings are a reminder of Gaudí's early training as a metalsmith (and he also designed much of the mansion's original furniture). The house is now open to the public – buy tickets online in advance.

Plaça de la Virreina

MAP P.121.
Ⓜ Fontana.

This pretty square, backed by the parish church of Sant Joan, is one of Gràcia's favourites, with a couple of bars providing a place to rest and admire the handsome houses, most notably the Casa Rubinat (1909).

Nearby streets, particularly **Carrer de Verdi**, contain many of the neighbourhood's most fashionable boutiques, galleries and cafés.

Verdi and Verdi Park

MAP P.121, POCKET MAP J1.
C/Verdi 32 and C/Torrijos 49. Ⓜ Fontana.
Ⓦ cines-verdi.com.

These art-house cinemas have sister locations in adjacent streets, with nine screens showing original-language movies from around the world. Tickets are priced highest at the weekend, cheaper through the week.

Plaça de la Vila de Gràcia

MAP P.121, POCKET MAP H1.
Ⓜ Diagonal.

The 30m-high clock tower in the heart of Gràcia was a rallying point for nineteenth-century radicals – whose twenty-first-century counterparts prefer to meet for brunch at the square's popular café *terrassas*.

Park Güell

MAP P.122, POCKET MAP K1.
C/d'Olot. Ⓜ Vallcarca/Lesseps.
Ⓦ parkguell.barcelona. Charge.

Gaudí's Park Güell (1900–14) was his most ambitious project after the Sagrada Família, conceived as a "garden city" of the type popular at the time in England, but opened as a public park instead in 1922. Laid out on a hill, which provides fabulous views back across the city, the park is an almost hallucinatory expression of the imagination. Pavilions of contorted stone, giant decorative lizards, meandering rustic viaducts, a vast Hall of Columns, carved stone trees – all combine in one manic swirl of ideas and excesses, like the famous ceramic bench that snakes along the edge of the terrace above the columned hall. Your ticket (advance bookings recommended) grants access to these sites, now part of the **monumental zone**.

Only 400 visitors are allowed inside this zone each half-hour. The area outside the monumental zone is free. Some areas might be closed due to restoration works.

The most direct route to Park Güell is on bus #24 from Plaça de Catalunya, Passeig de Gràcia or Carrer Gran de Gràcia, which drops you at the eastern side gate. From Ⓜ Vallcarca, walk a few hundred metres down Avinguda de Vallcarca until you see the mechanical escalators on your left, ascending Baixada de la Glòria – follow these to the western-side park entrance (15min in total). From Ⓜ Lesseps, turn right along Travessera de Dalt and then left up steep Carrer de Larrard, which leads (10min) straight to the main entrance on Carrer d'Olot.

Casa Museu Gaudí

MAP P.122, POCKET MAP K1.
Park Güell. Ⓜ Vallcarca/Lesseps.

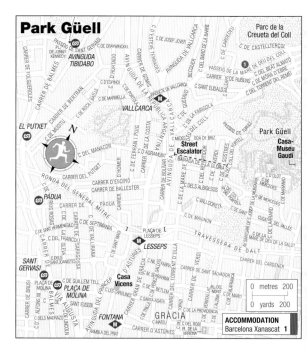

ACCOMMODATION
Barcelona Xanascat 1

Casa Museu Gaudí

 **casamuseugaudi.org. Charge, combination ticket with Sagrada Família available.**

One of Gaudí's collaborators, Francesc Berenguer, designed and built a turreted house within Park Güell for the architect (though he only lived in it intermittently). This contains a diverting collection of some of the furniture Gaudí designed for other projects – a typical mixture of wild originality and brilliant engineering – as well as plans and objects related to the park and to Gaudí's life. His study and bedroom have been preserved and there's an inkling of his personality, too, in the displayed religious texts and pictures, along with a silver coffee cup and his death mask, made at the Santa Pau hospital where he died.

Parc de la Creueta del Coll

MAP P.122, POCKET MAP K1.
Pg. de la Mare de Deu del Coll 89.
Ⓜ Vallcarca. Free.

For a different kind of experience altogether, combine a trip to Gaudí's extravagant Park Güell with this contemporary urban space laid out on the site of an old quarry, whose sheer walls were retained in the landscaping. You're greeted at the top of the park steps by an Ellsworth Kelly metal spike, while suspended by steel cables over water is a massive concrete claw by the Basque artist Eduardo Chillida. There are also palms, promenades and a kiosk-café.

Bus #V17 from near Plaça de Catalunya at Via Laietana and Ⓜ Urquinaona, stops 100m from the park, or you can walk from Ⓜ Vallcarca in about twenty minutes (there's a map of the neighbourhood at the metro station). It's worth knowing that if you visit Creueta del Coll first and then take the main Passeig de la Mare de Deu del Coll, there are signposts leading you into Park Güell the back way.

Hibernian Books

Shop

Hibernian Books

MAP P.121, POCKET MAP H1.
C/Montseny 17. Ⓜ Fontana.
Ⓦ hibernianbooks.com.
Barcelona's only secondhand
English bookstore has around
40,000 titles in stock – you can
part-exchange, and there are
always plenty of giveaway bargains
available.

Cafés

Deliziosa Gelateria Italiana

MAP P.121, POCKET MAP H1.
Pl. de la Revolució 2. Ⓜ Fontana.
Ⓦ gelateriaitalianadeliziosa.com.
Stroll around a pretty square in
the sun with a real hand-made
Italian ice cream (they've been
churning it out since 1881).
Expect queues at peak times, and
then more waiting as you struggle
to choose from the twenty-odd
flavours. €

La Nena

MAP P.121, POCKET MAP J1.
C/Ramon i Cajal 36, Ⓜ Joanic,
Ⓦ bit.ly/LaNenaB.
Great for home-made cakes,
waffles, quiches, organic ice
cream, squeezed juices and the
like. But parents also like the
"little girl" as it's very child-
friendly, from the changing mats
in the loos to the small seats,
games and puzzles. €

Restaurants and tapas bars

L'Arrosseria Xàtiva

MAP P.121, POCKET MAP J1.
C/Torrent d'en Vidalet 26. Ⓜ Joanic.
Ⓦ grupxativa.com.
The microwaved and burnt
offerings that pass for paella in
most Barcelona restaurants enrage
proud Valencians. For the real
thing, try one of the two *Xàtiva*
restaurants (the other is in Les
Corts). There's also a full range
of Catalan rice dishes including
creamy *arròs melòs*, and the lunch
menu is a great way to fill up before
exploring the area. €€€

Cal Boter

MAP P.121, POCKET MAP J1.
C/Tordera 62. Ⓜ Verdaguer.
Ⓦ restaurantcalboter.com.
This old-school bistro is perpetually
packed with people of all ages.
Survive the queue (or arrive when
it opens) and you'll be rewarded
with rib-sticking stews, meatballs,
snails and other classic dishes at
knockdown prices. €€

Flash, Flash

MAP P.121, POCKET MAP G1.
C/de la Granada del Penedès 25.
Ⓜ Diagonal. Ⓦ flashflashbarcelona.com.
A classic 1970s survivor with a
keen sense of style, *Flash, Flash*
does tortillas served any time you
like, any way you like, from plain
and simple to elaborately stuffed,

with sweet ones for dessert. If that doesn't grab you, try the reasonably priced salads, steaks, burgers and fish. The original white leatherette booths and monotone photo-model cut-outs are very Austin Powers. €

Nou Candanchu

MAP P.121, POCKET MAP H1.
Pl. de la Vila de Gràcia 9. Ⓜ Diagonal.
Ⓦ nou-candanchu.business.site.
Good for lunch on a sunny day or a leisurely night out on a budget, when you can sit beneath the clock tower and soak up the atmosphere in the ever-entertaining local square. There's a wide menu – tapas and hot sandwiches, but also steak and eggs, steamed clams and mussels, or cod and hake cooked plenty of different ways. €€

La Pepita

MAP P.121, POCKET MAP H2.
C/Còrsega 343. Ⓜ Diagonal/Verdaguer.
Ⓦ lapepitabcn.com.
There's usually a queue out the door here, and deservedly so. The tapas, such as Carabinero prawn croquettes with romesco sauce or smoked aubergine fritters with goats' cheese, honey and apples, are fantastic, and the atmosphere is chatty and convivial. Hundreds of "love notes" scrawled by customers on the white-tiled walls hint at its popularity. It's a good place for a drink if you show up outside kitchen hours too. €€

San Kil

MAP P.121, POCKET MAP H1.
Carrer de Legalitat 22. Ⓜ Joanic.
Ⓦ instagram.com/restaurante_san_kil.
There's no shortage of Korean restaurants in Barcelona, but *San Kil* has a place in the hearts of locals as the original. Family-run and super friendly, it's a no-nonsense affair, but the *bulgogi* (spicy beef wrapped in lettuce leaves), dumplings and seafood omelette are all excellent. €€

Bars

Bobby Gin

MAP P.121. POCKET MAP H1.
C/de Francisco Giner 47. Ⓜ Diagonal.
Ⓦ bobbygin.com.
The sign near the bar says "*El gintonic perfecto no existe*" (the perfect gin and tonic does not exist). Perhaps, but the sizeable G&Ts here, which come in a myriad of forms and flavours, come very, very close.

Café Salambo

MAP P.121, POCKET MAP K1.
C/Torrijos 51. Ⓜ Fontana.
Ⓦ cafesalambo.com.
Where the pre- and post-cinema crowd meets – both Verdi cinemas are on the doorstep. It's a long-standing spacious neighbourhood café, with something of a colonial feel, and there are lots of wines and cava by the glass, and good food too

Flash, Flash

Café del Sol

MAP P.121, POCKET MAP H1.
Pl. del Sol 16. Ⓜ Fontana. ☎ 932 371 448.
The grandaddy of the Plaça del Sol scene sees action day and night. On summer evenings, when the square is packed with people, there's not an outdoor table to be had, but even in winter this is a popular drinking den – the pubby interior has a back room and gallery, often rammed to the rafters.

Canigó

MAP P.121, POCKET MAP H1.
C/Verdi 2. Ⓜ Fontana. Ⓦ barcanigo.com.
Family-run neighbourhood bar now entering its third generation and second century. It's not much to look at, but the drinks are cheap and it's a Gràcia institution with a loyal following, packed out at weekends especially, with a young, largely local crowd.

Heliogabal

MAP P.121, POCKET MAP J1.
C/Ramon i Cajal 80 Ⓜ Joanic
Ⓦ heliogabal.com.
Not much more than a boiler room given a lick of paint, but filled

Café del Sol

with a cool, twenty-something crowd, here for the live poetry and music – expect something different every night (Catalan versifying, jazz jam sessions and earnest singer-songwriters), starting at 10pm. Admission varies, depending on the act, and drinks aren't expensive.

Old Fashioned

MAP P.121, POCKET MAP H2.
C/Santa Teresa 1. Ⓜ Diagonal.
Ⓦ bit.ly/OFBar.
Step inside and back in time to the Roaring Twenties, with waiters in white tuxes, old-school decor and a swinging soundtrack. The expert bartenders will mix a perfect classic cocktail or something more modern.

Vinil

MAP P.121, POCKET MAP H1.
C/Matilde 2. Ⓜ Diagonal.
Ⓦ facebook.com/barvinilbcn.
Wear a beret? Surgically attached to your iPad? Favour *Blade Runner*, Jeff Buckley and Band of Horses? This bar's for you – a dive bar with the lighting set at perpetual dusk, where time slips easily away.

Singer-songwriter Maria Coma performing at the Centre Artesà Tradicionàrius

Virreina

MAP P.121, POCKET MAP K1.
Pl. de la Virreina 1. ⓜ Fontana.
ⓣ 934 153 209.
Another real Gràcia favourite,
on one of the neighbourhood's
prettiest squares, with a very
popular summer *terrassa*. Cold
beer and sandwiches are served
to a laidback crowd – it's one of
those places where you drop by
for a quick drink and find yourself
staying for hours.

Clubs

Centre Artesà Tradicionàrius (CAT)

MAP P.121, POCKET MAP H1.
Trav. de Sant Antoni 6–8. ⓜ Fontana.
ⓦ tradicionarius.cat.
The best place in town for folk,
traditional and world music by
Catalan, Spanish and visiting
performers, including some
occasional big names. Admission
charges vary, and you can expect
anything from Basque bagpipes
to Brazilian singers. There are
also music and instrument
workshops, while CAT sponsors
all sorts of outreach concerts and
festivals, including an annual
international folk and traditional
dance festival between January
and April.

Otto Zutz

MAP P.121, POCKET MAP H1.
C/de Lincoln 15. ⓜ Fontana.
ⓦ ottozutz.com.
First opened in 1985, it has lost
some of its erstwhile glam cachet,
but this three-storey former
textile factory still has a shedload
of pretensions. The sounds are
basically hip-hop, r'n'b and house,
and with the right clothes and
face you're in (you may or may
not have to pay, depending on
how impressive you are, the day
of the week, the mood of the door
staff, etc).

Camp Nou, Pedralbes and Sarrià-Sant Gervasi

On the northwestern edge of the centre, the city's famous football stadium, Camp Nou, draws locals and visitors alike, both to the big game and to the FC Barcelona museum. Nearby, across Avinguda Diagonal, the Palau Reial de Pedralbes is home to serene public gardens (the lush vegetation hides an early work by Gaudí), while a half-day's excursion can be made by walking from the palace, past the Gaudí dragon gate at Pavellons Güell, to the calm cloister at the Gothic monastery of Pedralbes. You can complete the day by returning via Sarrià, to the east, more like a small town than a suburb, with a pretty main street and market to explore. At night, the focus shifts to the bars and restaurants of neighbouring Sant Gervasi in the streets north of Plaça de Francesc Macià.

Avinguda Diagonal

MAP P.130.
Ⓜ Maria Cristina.

The uptown section of Avinguda Diagonal runs through the heart of Barcelona's flashiest business and shopping district. The giant **L'Illa** shopping centre flanks the avenue – the stepped design is a prone echo of New York's

Camp Nou

Rockefeller Center. Designer fashion stores are ubiquitous, particularly around **Plaça de Francesc Macià** and Avinguda Pau Casals – at the end of the latter, **Turó Parc** is a good place to rest weary feet, with a small children's playground and a café-kiosk. Meanwhile, behind L'Illa, it's worth seeking out **Plaça de la Concordia**, a surprising survivor from the past amid the uptown tower blocks – the pretty little square is dominated by its church bell tower and ringed by local businesses (florist, pharmacy, hairdresser), with an outdoor café or two for a quiet drink.

Camp Nou and FC Barcelona

MAP P.130.
Av. Arístides Maillol. Ⓜ Collblanc/Maria Cristina. Ⓦ fcbarcelona.com. Match tickets also from Ⓦ ticketmaster.es.

In Barcelona, football is a genuine obsession, with support for the local giants FC (Futbol Club) Barcelona raised to an art form. "More than just a club" is the proud boast, and during the dictatorship years the club stood as a Catalan symbol around which people could rally. Arch rivals, Real Madrid, on the other hand, were always seen as Franco's club. The swashbuckling team – past European champions and darling of football neutrals everywhere – plays at the magnificent Camp Nou football stadium, built in 1957, and enlarged for the 1982 World Cup semifinal to accommodate 98,000 spectators. A new remodelling (by architect Norman Foster) plans to update the stadium over the next few years, but even today Camp Nou provides one of the world's best football-watching experiences.

The **football season** runs from August until May, with league games usually played on Sundays. Tickets are relatively easy to come by, except for the biggest games,

FC Barcelona Museu

and go on general sale up to a month before each match – buy them online or at the ticket office.

The stadium complex hosts basketball, handball and hockey games with FC Barcelona's other professional teams, and there's also a public ice rink, souvenir shop and café.

Camp Nou Experience

MAP P.130.
Camp Nou, Av. Arístides Maillol, enter through Gates 7 & 9. Ⓜ Collblanc/Maria Cristina. Ⓦ fcbarcelona.com. Charge.

No soccer fan should miss the Camp Nou stadium tour and museum, billed as the "Camp Nou Experience". The self-guided tour winds through the changing rooms, onto the pitch and up to the press gallery and directors' box for stunning views. The museum, meanwhile, is jammed full of silverware and memorabilia, while displays and archive footage trace the history of the club back to 1901. Finally, you're directed into the massive **FC Botiga**, where you can buy anything from a replica shirt to a branded bottle of wine.

Camp Nou, Pedralbes and Sarrià-Sant Gervasi

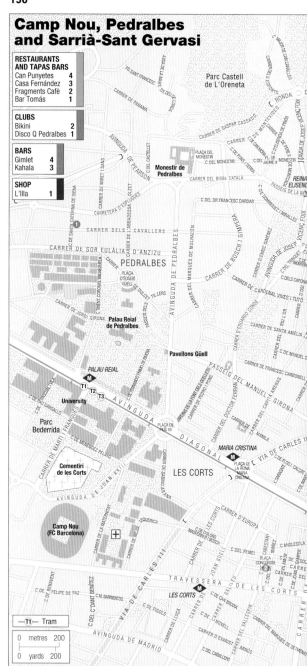

RESTAURANTS AND TAPAS BARS
Can Punyetes 4
Casa Fernández 3
Fragments Cafè 2
Bar Tomás 1

CLUBS
Bikini 2
Disco Q Pedralbes 1

BARS
Gimlet 4
Kahala 3

SHOP
L'Illa 1

—T1— Tram

0   metres   200
0   yards   200

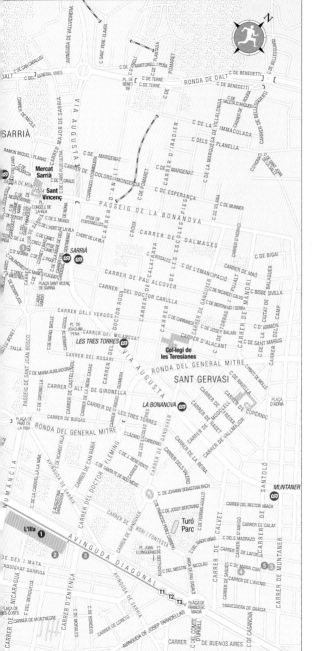

Palau Reial de Pedralbes

the palace somewhat lost its role. Franco kept it on as a presidential residence and it later passed to the city. The rooms had been used to show off the city's applied art collections, but those collections have since moved to the Museu del Disseny near Plaça de les Glòries Catalanes. Although the palace is now closed to the public, the gardens – a breezy oasis of Himalaya cedar, strawberry trees and bougainvillea – are worth a visit. Hidden in a bamboo thicket, to the left-centre of the facade, is the "Hercules fountain" (1884), an early work by Antoni Gaudí. He also designed the parabolic pergola, which is covered in climbing plants and is a nice place to sit and rest your feet. In late June, a music festival (Ⓦ festivalpedralbes.com) takes place in the palace's gardens.

Palau Reial de Pedralbes

MAP P.130.
Av. Diagonal 686. Ⓜ Palau Reial. Free.
Opposite the university on Avinguda Diagonal, formal grounds stretch up to the Italianate Palau Reial de Pedralbes – basically a large villa with pretensions. It was built for the use of the royal family on their visits to Barcelona, with funds raised by public subscription, and received its first such visit in 1926. However, within five years the king had abdicated and

Pavellons Güell

MAP P.130.
Av. de Pedralbes 7. Ⓜ Palau Reial.
Ⓦ bit.ly/PavGuell. Charge.
As an early test of his capabilities, Antoni Gaudí was asked by his patron, Eusebi Güell, to rework the entrance, gatehouse and stables of the Güell summer residence. The resultant brick and tile buildings are frothy, whimsical affairs, though it's the gateway that's the most famous element. An extraordinary winged dragon

Here be dragons

The slavering beast on Gaudí's dragon gate at the Pavellons Güell is not the vanquished dragon of Sant Jordi (St George), the Catalan patron saint, but the one that appears in the Labours of Hercules myth, a familiar Catalan theme in the nineteenth century. Gaudí's design was based on a work by the Catalan renaissance poet Jacint Verdaguer, a friend of the Güell family, who had reworked the myth in his epic poem, *L'Atlàntida* – thus, the dragon guarding golden apples in the Gardens of Hesperides is here protecting instead an orange tree (considered a more Catalan fruit). Gaudí's gate indeed can be read as an homage to Verdaguer, with its stencilled roses representing those traditionally given to the winner of the Catalan poetry competition, the Jocs Floral, which the poet won in 1877.

of twisted iron snarls at passers-by, its razor-toothed jaws spread wide in a fearsome roar. Guided visits show you the grounds and Gaudí's innovative stables, now used as a library by the university's historical architecture department.

Sarrià

MAP P.130.
FGC Sarrià, or bus #64 from Pl. Universitat or Pedralbes.

The Sarrià district was once an independent small town and still looks the part, with a narrow, traffic-free main street – Carrer Major de Sarrià – at the top of which stands the much-restored church of Sant Vicenç. The church flanks the main Passeig de la Reina Elisenda de Montcada, across which lies the neighbourhood market, Mercat Sarrià, housed in a 1911 *modernista* red-brick building. You'll find a few other surviving old-town squares down the main street, prettiest of which is Plaça Sant Vicenç de Sarrià (off Carrer de Mañe i Flaquer), where there's a statue of the saint.

Monestir de Pedralbes

Monestir de Pedralbes

MAP P.130.
Baixada del Monestir. Ⓜ Palau Reial and 20min walk, or FGC Reina Elisenda and 10min walk, or bus #63 from Pl. Universitat. Ⓦ monestirpedralbes.barcelona. Charge, free first Sun of the month.

Founded in 1326 for the nuns of the Order of St Clare, this is in effect an entire monastic village set within medieval walls on the outskirts of the city. The cloisters in particular are the finest in Barcelona, built on three levels and adorned by the slenderest of columns. Side rooms and chambers give a clear impression of medieval convent life, and also display a selection of the monastery's treasures, while the adjacent church contains the carved marble tomb of the convent's founder, Elisenda de Montcada, wife of King Jaume II. After 600 years of isolation, the monastery was sequestered by the Generalitat during the Civil War. It was turned into a museum in 1983, and a new adjacent convent was built, where the Clare nuns still reside.

CAMP NOU, PEDRALBES AND SARRIÀ-SANT GERVASI

Shop

L'Illa

MAP P.130.
Av. Diagonal 555–559. Ⓜ Maria Cristina.
Ⓦ lilla.com.

The landmark uptown shopping mall is stuffed full of designer fashion, plus Camper (shoes), FNAC (music, film and books), Decathlon (sports), El Corte Inglés (department store), Caprabo (supermarket), food hall and much more. You can get here by metro or tram (from Pl. de Francesc Macià).

Restaurants and tapas bars

Can Punyetes

MAP P.130.
C/Marià Cubí 189. FGC Muntaner.
Ⓦ canpunyetesbarcelona.com.

Traditional grillhouse-tavern that offers diners a taste of older times. Simple salads and tapas, open grills turning out *botifarra* (sausage), lamb chops, chicken and pork – accompanied by grilled country bread, white beans and chargrilled potato halves. It's cheap and locals love it. €

Casa Fernández

MAP P.130.
C/Santaló 46. FGC Muntaner.
Ⓦ casafernandez.com.

The long kitchen hours are a boon for the bar-crawlers in this neck of the woods. It's a contemporary place featuring market cuisine, though they are specialists in – of all things – fried eggs, either served straight with chips or with Catalan sausage, garlic prawns or other variations. €€

Fragments Cafè

MAP P.130.
Pl. de la Concòrdia 12. Ⓜ Les Corts.
Ⓦ fragmentscafe.com.

L'Illa

A classy yet casual bistro popular with locals for its fresh, classic food that's served in the charming dining room or in the shaded garden. Main courses include salmon tartar, grilled sea bass and glazed beef cheek, and there's a list of hot and cold tapas. €€

Bar Tomás

MAP P.130.
C/Major de Sarrià 49. FGC Sarrià.
W eltomasdesarria.com.

The best *patatas bravas* in Barcelona? Everyone will point you here, to this unassuming, white-Formica-table bar in the suburbs (a 12min train ride from Plaça de Catalunya FGC) for their unrivalled spicy fried potatoes with garlic mayo and *salsa picante*. It's not all they serve, but it might as well be. They fry noon to 3pm and 6pm to closing, so if it's *patatas bravas* you want, be sure to take a note of the hours. €

Bars

Gimlet

MAP P.130.
C/Santaló 46. FGC Muntaner.
W gimletbcn.com.

This favoured cocktail joint is especially popular in summertime, when the streetside tables offer a great vantage point for watching the party unfold. There are also two or three other late-opening bars on the same stretch.

Kahala

MAP P.130.
Avgda. Diagonal 537. W Maria Cristina.
W kahalabarcelona.com.

Open since 1971, this Hawaiian-themed bar is a treasure-trove of Polynesian kitsch: gurgling waterfalls, bamboo furniture and grimacing tiki masks abound. The drinks – from the Perla de Vicio ("Pearl of Vice") to the classic Mai Tai – pack quite the punch and are certain to ready you for an evening of clubbing.

Gimlet

Clubs

Bikini

MAP P.130.
C/Deu i Mata 105. W Les Corts/Maria Cristina. W bikinibcn.com.

This traditional landmark of Barcelona nightlife (behind the L'Illa shopping centre) offers a regular diet of great indie, rock, roots and world gigs followed by club sounds, from house to Brazilian, according to the night. Admission charges vary.

Disco Q Pedralbes

MAP P.130.
C/Santa Caterina de Siena 28. W Passeig de Gracia es Corts. W discoqpedralbes.com.

Offers pop and rock'n'roll or live music on Thursdays, eighties and nineties hits on Fridays and Saturdays, and eighties disco fever on Sundays. On Fridays and Saturdays "dinner + disco" is available, though you'll do better eating elsewhere.

Tibidabo and Parc de Collserola

The views from the heights of Tibidabo (550m), the peak that signals the northwestern boundary of the city, are legendary. On a clear day you can see across to the Pyrenees and out to sea even as far as Mallorca. However, while many make the tram and funicular ride up to Tibidabo's amusement park, few realize that beyond stretches the Parc de Collserola, an area of peaks, wooded river valleys and hiking paths – one of Barcelona's best-kept secrets. You can walk into the park from Tibidabo, but it's actually better to start from the park's information centre, across to the east above Vallvidrera, where hiking-trail leaflets are available. Meanwhile, families won't want to miss CosmoCaixa, the city's excellent science museum, which can easily be seen on the way to or from Tibidabo.

Parc d'Atraccions

MAP P.137.
Pl. del Tibidabo. Ⓦ tibidabo.cat. Charge.
Barcelona's self-styled "magic mountain" amusement park takes full advantage of its hillside location to offer jaw-dropping perspectives over the city. Some of the most famous rides, such as the iconic aeroplane, have been running since the 1920s. All tickets include transport on the new funicular train ('Cuca de Llum') to get up here from Plaça Doctor Andreu. Summer weekends finish with parades,

Parc d'Atraccions

concerts and a noisy *correfoc*, a theatrical fireworks display.

Sagrat Cor

MAP P.137.

Ⓦ tibidabo.salesianos.edu. Free, charge for elevator.

Next to Tibidabo's amusement park climb the shining steps of the Templo Expiatorio de España – otherwise known as the Sagrat Cor (Sacred Heart). This is topped by a huge statue of Christ, and inside the church an elevator (10am–2pm & 3–7pm) climbs to a viewing platform from where the city, surrounding hills and shimmering sea glisten in the distance.

Torre de Collserola

MAP P.137.

Carretera de Vallvidrera al Tibidabo.
Ⓦ torredecollserola.com. Charge.
Follow the road from the Tibidabo car park and it's only a few minutes' walk to Norman Foster's

soaring communications tower, built for the 1992 Olympics. This features a glass elevator that whisks you up ten storeys (115m) for extensive views – 70km, they claim, on a good day. Note that there's a combo ticket for the tower available at the Tibidabo amusement park.

Parc de Collserola

MAP P.137.

Centre d'Informació, FGC Baixada de Vallvidrera (on the Sabadell or Terrassa line from Pl. de Catalunya; 15min).
Ⓦ parcnaturalcollserola.cat. Free.
Given a half-decent day, local bikers, hikers and outdoor enthusiasts all make a beeline for the city's ring of wooded hills beyond Tibidabo. The park information centre lies in oak and pine woods, an easy ten-minute walk up through the trees from the FGC Baixada de Vallvidrera train station. There's a bar-restaurant

TIBIDABO AND PARC DE COLLSEROLA

Getting to Tibidabo

Reaching the heights of Tibidabo takes up to an hour, all told, from the city centre. First, take the FGC train (line 7) from Plaça de Catalunya station to **Avinguda Tibidabo** (the last stop), where you cross the road to the tram/bus shelter (the Bus Turístic stops here too). The **Tramvia Blau**, an antique tram service, was closed for restoration at the time of writing, but a replacement bus runs you up the hill to Plaça Doctor Andreu. Here, you change to the Cuca de Llum ('Glowworm') funicular railway, with connections every 15min to Tibidabo (ⓦ tibidabo.cat/cucadellum, included in price of funfair ticket or available separately). Alternatively, the **Tibibus** runs direct to Tibidabo from Plaça Kennedy (included in funfair admission).

here with an outdoor terrace, plus an exhibition on the park's history, flora and fauna, while the staff hand out English-language leaflets detailing the various park walks. Some of the well-marked paths – like the oak-forest walk – soon gain height for marvellous views over the tree canopy, while others descend through the valley bottoms to springs and shaded picnic areas. Perhaps the nicest short walk from the information centre is to the **Font de la Budellera** (1hr 15min return), a landscaped spring deep in the woods. If you follow the

signs from the *font* to the Torre de Collserola (another 20min), you can return to Barcelona on the funicular from the nearby suburban village of **Vallvidrera**, which connects to Peu del Funicular, an FGC train station on the line from Plaça de Catalunya.

Museu-Casa Verdaguer
MAP P.137.
Villa Joana, Carretera de l'Església 104.
ⓦ verdaguer.cat. Free.
If you're up at the park, it's worth having a quick look inside the country house just below the

Parc de Collserola

CosmoCaixa

Collserola information centre. Jacint Verdaguer (1845–1902), the Catalan Renaissance poet, lived here briefly before his death, and the house has been preserved as an example of well-to-do nineteenth-century Catalan life.

CosmoCaixa

MAP P.137.
C/Isaac Newton 26. ⓦ cosmocaixa.com.
Charge.

A dramatic refurbishment in 2005 turned the city's science museum into a must-see attraction, certainly if you've got children in tow – it's an easy place to spend a couple of hours and can break the journey on your way to or from Tibidabo. Partly housed in a converted *modernista* hospice, the museum retains the original building but has added a light-filled public concourse and a huge underground extension with four subterranean levels, where hands-on experiments and displays investigate life, the universe and everything, "from bacteria to Shakespeare". The two big draws are the hundred tonnes of "sliced rock" in the Geological Wall and, best of all, the Bosc Inundat – nothing less than a thousand square metres of real Amazonian rainforest, complete with croc-filled mangroves, anacondas and giant catfish. Other levels of the museum are devoted to children's and family activities, which tend to be held at weekends and during school holidays; pick up a schedule when you arrive. There are daily shows in the planetarium (in Spanish and Catalan only), a great gift shop and a café-restaurant with outdoor seating.

The easiest way to reach CosmoCaixa is by FGC train from Plaça de Catalunya to Avinguda del Tibidabo station, and then walk up the avenue, turning left just before the ring road (10min) – or the Tramvia Blau or Bus Turístic can drop you close by.

Bar

Mirablau

MAP P.137.
Pl. del Dr. Andreu, Av. Tibidabo
ⓦ mirablaubcn.cat.

Unbelievable city views from a chic bar near the Tibidabo funicular that fills to bursting at times. By day, a great place for coffee, by night a rich-kid disco-tunes stomping ground.

Montserrat

The mountain of Montserrat, with its rock crags, vast monastery and hermitage caves, stands just 40km northwest of Barcelona. It's the most popular day trip from the city, reached in around ninety minutes by train and then cable car or rack railway for a thrilling ride up to the monastery. Once there, you can visit the basilica and monastery buildings and complete your day with a walk around the woods and crags, using the two funicular railways that depart from the complex. There are cafés and restaurants at the monastery, but they are relatively pricey and none too inspiring – you may wish to take a picnic instead.

Aeri de Montserrat

MAP P.140.
Montserrat Aeri. Ⓦ aeridemontserrat.com.
For the cable car service, get off the train from Barcelona at Aeri de Montserrat station (around one hour). You may have to wait in line fifteen minutes or so, but then it's only a five-minute swoop up the sheer mountainside to a terrace just below the monastery – probably the most exhilarating ride in Catalunya. Returning to Barcelona, the line R5 trains depart one or twice an hour from Aeri de Montserrat.

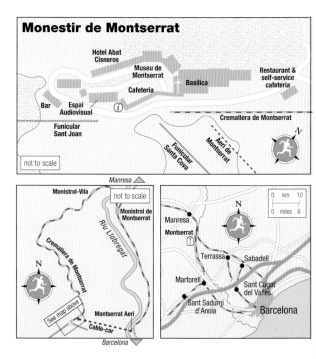

Cremallera de Montserrat

MAP P.140.

Monistrol de Montserrat.

Ⓦ cremallerademontserrat.com.

The alternative approach to the monastery is by the Montserrat rack railway, which departs from Monistrol de Montserrat station (the next stop after Montserrat Aeri, another 4min), and takes twenty minutes to complete the climb. The original rack railway on Montserrat ran between 1892 and 1957, and this modern replacement re-creates the majestic engineering that allows the train to climb 550m in 4km. Returning to Barcelona, the line R5 trains depart at least hourly from Monistrol de Montserrat.

Monestir de Montserrat

MAP P.140.

Visitor centre. Ⓦ montserratvisita.com. Walking maps and accommodation advice available. Charge.

Legends hang easily upon the monastery of Montserrat. Fifty years after the birth of Christ, St Peter is said to have deposited an image of the Virgin (known as La Moreneta), carved by St Luke, in one of the mountain caves. The icon was lost in the early eighth century after being hidden during the Moorish invasion, but reappeared in 880, accompanied by the customary visions and celestial music. A chapel was built to house it, and in 976 this was superseded by a Benedictine

Monestir de Montserrat

monastery, set at an altitude of nearly 1000m. Miracles abounded and the Virgin of Montserrat soon became the chief cult image of Catalunya and a pilgrimage centre second in Spain only to Santiago de Compostela – the main pilgrimages to Montserrat take place on April 27 and September 8.

The monastery's various outbuildings – including hotel,

Getting to Montserrat

To reach the Montserrat cable car/rack railway stations, take the **FGC train** (line R5, direction Manresa), which leaves daily from **Plaça d'Espanya** (Ⓦ Espanya) at hourly intervals from 5am. All fare options are detailed at Plaça d'Espanya, including return through-tickets from Barcelona either for the train/cable car or train/rack railway. There are also combination tickets such as the **Tot Montserrat** (Ⓦ totmontserrat.com), which also includes the monastery museum, the rack railway at the monastery itself and a cafeteria lunch. Tickets are also available at the Plaça de Catalunya tourist office.

post office, souvenir shop and bar – fan out around an open square, and there are extraordinary mountain views from the terrace. The best restaurant is inside the *Hotel Abat Cisneros*, though the finest views are from the mediocre self-service cafeteria where you eat with the all-inclusive *Tot Montserrat* ticket.

Basílica

MAP P.140.
Free.

Of the religious buildings, only the Renaissance basilica, dating largely from 1560 to 1592, is open to the public. **La Moreneta** stands above the high altar – reached from behind, by way of an entrance to the right of the basilica's main entrance. The approach to this beautiful icon reveals the enormous wealth of the monastery, as you queue along a corridor leading through the back of the basilica's rich side chapels. Signs at head height command "SILENCE" in various languages, but nothing quietens the line which waits to kiss the image's hands and feet.

The best time to be here is when Montserrat's world-famous **boys' choir** sings (Mon–Fri 1pm; performance times may vary during school holidays at Christmas/New Year and from late June to mid-August). The boys belong to the Escolania, a choral school established in the thirteenth century and unchanged in musical style since its foundation.

Museu de Montserrat

MAP P.140.
Ⓦ museudemontserrat.com. Charge.

The monastery museum presents a few archeological finds brought back by travelling monks, together with valuable painting

Basílica, Monestir de Montserrat

Funicular, Montserrat

and sculpture dating from the thirteenth century onwards, including works by Old Masters, French Impressionists and Catalan *modernistas*. There's also a collection of Byzantine icons, though other religious items are in surprisingly short supply, as most of the monastery's valuables were carried off by Napoleon's troops who sacked the complex in 1811. For more on the history, and to learn something of the life of a Benedictine community, visit the **Espai Audiovisual** (charge), near the information office.

Mountain walks

Following the mountain tracks to the caves and hermitages, you can contemplate Goethe's observation of 1816: "Nowhere but in his own Montserrat will a man find happiness and peace." The going is pretty good on all the tracks and the signposting is clear, but you do need to remember that you are on a mountain. Take water if you're hiking far and keep away from the edges.

Two separate funiculars run from points close to the cable car station. One drops to the path for **Santa Cova**, a seventeenth-century chapel built where the Moreneta icon is said to have been found. It's an easy walk of less than an hour there and back. The other funicular rises steeply to the hermitage of **Sant Joan**, from where it's a tougher 45 minutes' walk to the **Sant Jeroni** hermitage, and another 15 minutes to the Sant Jeroni summit at 1236m. Several other walks are also possible from the Sant Joan funicular, perhaps the nicest being the 45-minute circuit around the ridge that leads all the way back down to the monastery.

Sitges

The seaside town of Sitges, 36km south of Barcelona, is definitely the highlight of the local coast – a great weekend escape for young Barcelonans, who have created a resort very much in their own image. It's also a noted gay holiday destination, with an outrageous annual carnival (February/March) and a summertime nightlife to match. During the heat of the day, though, the tempo drops as everyone hits the beach. Out of season, Sitges is delightful: far less crowded, and with a temperate climate that encourages promenade strolls and Old Town exploration.

The beaches

MAP P.145.

There are clean sands on either side of the Old Town, though they become extremely crowded in high season. For more space keep walking west from Passeig de la Ribera along Passeig Marítim promenade, past eight interlinked beaches that run a couple of kilometres down the coast as far as the *Hotel Terramar*. Many of the handsome, nineteenth-century seafront mansions were built by successful local merchants (known as "Americanos") who had returned from Cuba and Puerto Rico.

The old town

MAP P.145.

The knoll overlooking the town beaches is topped by the landmark Baroque parish church dedicated to Sant Bartolomeu, whose festival is celebrated in the last week of August. The views from the terrace sweep along the coast, while behind in the narrow

The picturesque seafront at Sitges.

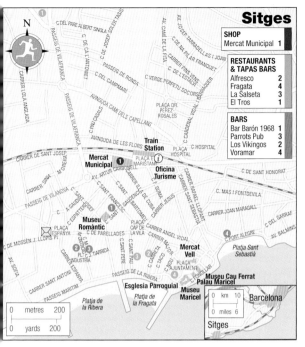

Sitges

SHOP	
Mercat Municipal	1

RESTAURANTS & TAPAS BARS	
Alfresco	2
Fragata	4
La Salseta	3
El Tros	1

BARS	
Bar Barón 1968	1
Parrots Pub	3
Los Vikingos	2
Voramar	4

streets of the Old Town you'll find whitewashed mansions, as well as the town hall and the **Mercat Vell** (Old Market), the latter now an exhibition hall. The pedestrianized shopping street, **Carrer Major**, is the best place for browsing boutiques.

Cau Ferrat, Maricel and Romàntico museums

MAP P.145.
Ⓦ museusdesitges.cat. Charge.

Three museums showcase the town's artistic heritage, not least the renovated **Museu Cau Ferrat** (Carrer de Fonollar), the former house of *modernista* artist Santiago Rusiñol (1861–1931). Next door, the **Museu de Maricel** contains minor artworks, ceramics and sculpture, while in July and August (usually two evenings a week) the main part of the mansion itself is open for guided tours and concerts. Occupying a

stately bourgeois house of 1793, the **Museu Romàntico** (Carrer de Sant Gaudenci 1) shows the lifestyle of a rich, nineteenth-century Sitges family.

Museu de Maricel

Rainbow flags and bunting for Sitges Pride

Shop

Mercat Municipal

MAP P.145.

Av. Artur Carbonell. Ⓦ mercatsitges.cat.
The town market is a great place
to put together a picnic of cured
meats, olives, cheese, fresh bread
and fruit.

Restaurants and tapas bars

Alfresco

MAP P.145.

C/Pau Barrabeig 4.
Ⓦ alfrescorestaurante.es.
Exuding romance – from its
tucked-away location off a stepped
alley to its trellised patio – this
restaurant serves Catalan cuisine
with Asian influences (green
Thai curry, duck breast with glass
noodles). €€

Fragata

MAP P.145.

Pg. de la Ribera 1.
Ⓦ restaurantefragata.com.
Fragata is typical of the new wave
of classy seafood places in town,
where catch-of-the-day choices
include grilled scallops or wild sea
bass. €€€

La Salseta

MAP P.145.

C/Sant Pau 35. Ⓦ lasalseta.com.
Classic, unpretentious Catalan
dishes (cod with garlic confit,
seafood paella) made from
locally sourced ingredients at
reasonable prices have kept this
old restaurant's cosy dining room
filled with both tourists and
locals. €€

El Tros

MAP P.145.

C/Sant Pere de Ribes 12. ☎ 938 110 696.
A little family-run restaurant
with a friendly atmosphere that
offers tasty food at very good
prices. Have a Spanish omelette
for breakfast or come to get some
lunch at around 1.30pm – try the
menú del día with some delicious
coffee. €

Sitges information

Trains to Sitges leave Passeig de Gràcia or Barcelona Sants
stations every twenty minutes, more frequently at peak times
(destination Vilanova/St Vicenç), and it's a thirty- to forty-minute
ride depending on the service. The main Oficina Turisme (Pl.
Eduard Maristany 2, Ⓦ sitgestur.cat) is adjacent to the train
station. Note that Monday isn't the best day to come, as the
museums and many restaurants are closed. As well as Carnival,
Sitges is known for its celebrated annual sci-fi, horror and fantasy
fest, the Festival Internacional de Cinema (Ⓦ sitgesfilmfestival.
com) every October.

The LGBTQ+ scene and Carnival

The Sitges LGBTQ+ scene is frenetic and ever-changing, but the bulk of the nightlife is centred on Plaça de l'Indústria. Summer, of course, sees one, long non-stop party, but Carnival time (Feb/March) is also notoriously riotous, with a full programme of parades, masked balls, concerts and beach parties. Highlights are Sunday night's Debauchery Parade and Tuesday's Extermination Parade, in which exquisitely dressed drag queens twirl lacy parasols, while bar doors stand wide open and the celebrations go on till dawn. The other big bash is Gay Pride Sitges (ⓦ gaypridesitges.com), a weekend of events plus a street parade every July.

Bars

Bar Barón 1968

MAP P.145.
C/Sant Gaudenci 17. ⓦ facebook.com/Bar.
Baron1968.

Definitely not a stylish bar, but this old tavern is a real slice of Sitges nonetheless. It's nowhere near the sea, so there's more of a down-to-earth local crowd.

Parrots Pub

MAP P.145.
Pl. de l'Indústria. ⓦ parrots-sitges.com.

The stalwart of the gay bar scene in Sitges, with front-row seats on all the action.

Carnival

Los Vikingos

MAP P.145.
C/Marqués de Montroig 7–9.
ⓦ losvikingos.com.

Long-standing party-zone bar with a huge air-conditioned interior and streetside terrace. This and the similar *Montroig* next door serve drinks, snacks and meals from morning until night to a really mixed crowd.

Voramar

MAP P.145.
C/Port Alegre 55. ⓦ pub-voramar.com.

Charismatic seafront bar, away from the main crowds, just right for an ice-cold beer or sundowner cocktail.

ACCOMMODATION

Hotel Arts Barcelona

Accommodation

Finding a hotel vacancy in Barcelona at any time of year can be very difficult, so it's best to book in advance. The absolute cheapest rooms in a simple family-run *hostal* or *pensión*, sharing a bathroom, cost around €60 (singles from €40), though if you want private facilities €70–80 a night is more realistic. There's a fair amount of choice over the €100 mark, while up to €250 gets you the run of decent hotels in most city areas. For Barcelona's most fashionable hotels count on €250–400 a night, while dorm beds in youth hostels go for €20 to €30 depending on the season. A ten-percent tax (IVA) is added to all accommodation bills (though it's sometimes included in the quoted price), and a "tourist tax" adds €2.75 to €6.25 per person per night to your bill for stays of up to seven days. Under-17s are exempt, and most tourist establishments in Barcelona fall into the lowest tax band. Breakfast isn't usually included, unless specifically stated in the reviews. Credit cards are accepted almost everywhere (though American Express isn't always). There's a lot of street noise in Barcelona, so bring earplugs if you're at all concerned.

Along La Rambla

EXE RAMBLAS BOQUERÍA MAP P.26, POCKET MAP C12. La Rambla 91–93. Ⓜ Liceu. Ⓦ exeramblasboqueria.com. Snappy little boutique rooms in a small three-star hotel right outside the Boqueria market. There's not much space, but all you need is on the doorstep, and the soundproofing is good so you get a street view without the racket. €€€

HOSTAL BENIDORM MAP P.26, POCKET MAP C13. La Rambla 37. Ⓜ Drassanes. Ⓦ hostalbenidorm.com. Refurbished *pensión* that offers real value for money, hence the tribes of young tourists. Rooms available for one to five people, and a balcony with a La Rambla view if you're lucky (and prepared to pay a bit more). €€

HOTEL 1898 MAP P.26, POCKET MAP C11. La Rambla 109. Ⓜ Catalunya. Ⓦ hotel1898.com. The former HQ of the Philippines Tobacco Company got an eye-popping boutique refit, adding four grades of rooms (the standard is "Classic") in deep red, green or black, plus sumptuous suites and dramatic public areas, including a neocolonial lobby-lounge bar, heated rooftop pool and glam spa facilities. €€€€

HOTEL ORIENTE MAP P.26, POCKET MAP C13. La Rambla 45. Ⓜ Liceu. Ⓦ atiramhotels.com. For somewhere on La Rambla that's traditional but not too pricey, this historic three-star hotel is your best bet – nineteenth-century style in the grand public rooms and tastefully updated bedrooms, some with La Rambla views (though the quieter ones face inwards). €€€

HOTEL RIVOLI RAMBLA MAP P.26, POCKET MAP D11. La Rambla 128. Ⓜ Catalunya. Ⓦ hotelserhsrivolirambla. com. The elegant rooms in this four-star hotel are imaginatively furnished (Art Deco to contemporary); all come with spacious bathrooms, while the front ones have floor-to-ceiling windows and classic views of La Rambla. There's a lovely rooftop terrace and bar. €€€

Barri Gòtic

HOTEL EL JARDÍ MAP P.34, POCKET MAP D12. Pl. Sant Josep Oriol 1. ⓜLiceu. ⓦeljardi-barcelona.com. Location is all – overlooking the charming Plaça del Pi – and though rooms can seem a bit bare and plain, some look directly onto the square (terrace or balcony rooms cost a little more). You can have breakfast at the hotel, though the *Bar del Pi* below is nicer. €€

HOTEL RACÓ DEL PI MAP P.34, POCKET MAP D12. C/del Pi 7. ⓜLiceu. ⓦhotelh10racodelpi.com. A stylish three-star hotel in a great location. Rooms – some with balconies over the street – have wood floors and granite-and-mosaic bathrooms. There's a glass of cava on check-in, and free coffee and pastries during the day in the bar. €€€

ITACA HOSTEL MAP P.34, POCKET MAP E12. C/Ripoll 21. ⓜJaume I. ⓦitacahostel.com. Bright and breezy hostel close to the

cathedral offering spacious rooms with balconies. Dorms are mixed, though you can also reserve a private room (sleeps up to three), and with a capacity of only 30, it feels more house party than hostel. €€

NERI HOTEL MAP P.34, POCKET MAP D12. C/de Sant Sever 5. ⓜLiceu/Jaume I. ⓦhotelneri.com. A delightful eighteenth-century palace close to the cathedral houses this stunning boutique hotel of just 22 rooms and suites, featuring swags of flowing material, rescued timber and granite-toned bathrooms. Catalan designers have created eye-catching effects, like a tapestry that falls four floors through the central atrium, while a beamed library and stylish roof terrace provide a tranquil escape. The "a" Restaurant downstairs serves excellent twists on Catalan and French cuisine. €€€€

PENSIÓ ALAMAR MAP P.34, POCKET MAP D13. C/Comtessa de Sobradiel 1. ⓜLiceu/Jaume I. ⓦpensioalamar.com. If you don't mind sharing a bathroom, this simply furnished *pensión* makes a convenient base. There are twelve rooms (including singles, doubles and triples), most with little balconies, and there's a friendly welcome, laundry service and use of a kitchen. €

What's the neighbourhood like?

If you hanker after a view of **La Rambla**, you'll pay for the privilege – generally speaking, there are better deals to be had either side of the famous boulevard, often just a minute's walk away. Alongside some classy boutique choices, most of Barcelona's cheapest accommodation is found in the Old Town, principally the **Barri Gòtic** and **El Raval** neighbourhoods, which both still have their rough edges – be careful (without being paranoid) when coming and going after dark. North of Plaça de Catalunya, the **Eixample** – split into Right (**Dreta**) and Left (**Esquerra**) – has some of the city's most fashionable hotels. Those near **Sants** station are convenient for onward train travel, and those further north in **Les Corts** for the Avinguda Diagonal shopping district. For waterfront views look at **Port Vell** at the end of La Rambla, and at the **Port Olímpic** southeast of the Old Town – while newer four- and five-star hotels abound further out on the metro at the **Diagonal Mar** conference and events site. If you prefer neighbourhood living then **Gràcia** is the best base, as you're only ever a short walk away from its excellent bars, restaurants and clubs.

Port Vell and Barceloneta

H10 PORT VELL MAP P.48, POCKET MAP D14. Pas de Sota Muralla 9. Ⓜ Barceloneta. Ⓦ h10hotels.com. An elegant hotel set in a restored historic building. On the rooftop there is a lovely terrace with a bar, a swimming pool and a gorgeous view of the port. Well located and close to many popular restaurants, it also has an excellent restaurant itself. €€€

HOTEL DUQUESA DE CARDONA MAP P.48, POCKET MAP D14. Pg. de Colom 12. Ⓜ Drassanes/Barceloneta. Ⓦ hduquesadecardona.com. Step off the busy harbourfront highway into this soothing four-star haven, set in a remodelled sixteenth-century mansion. The rooms are calm and quiet, decorated in earth tones and immaculately appointed. Although not all of the rooms have harbour views, all guests have access to the stylish roof-deck overlooking the harbour. It's great for sundowner drinks, and has a small pool. €€€

SEA HOSTEL MAP P.48, POCKET MAP H8. Pl. del Mar 1–4. Ⓜ Barceloneta. Ⓦ seahostelbarcelona.com. The budget beachside choice is this neat little hostel with modern en-suite rooms sleeping four to eight people. The attached café looks right out onto the boardwalk. €€

SERRAS HOTEL MAP P.48, POCKET MAP D14. Passeig de Colom 9. Ⓜ Barceloneta. Ⓦ serrashotel.com. A breezy, elegant hotel that manages to be smart but relaxed. Rooms feature vast beds and lots of crushed velvet – book a room at the front for a view across the port. The rooftop restaurant is great for a Mediterranean lunch, and you can slide into the small pool afterwards. €€€€

W BARCELONA MAP P.48, POCKET MAP G9. Pl. de la Rosa dels Vents. Ⓜ Barceloneta. Ⓦ w-barcelona.com. The signature (but controversial) building on the Barceloneta seafront is the W Barcelona. No one calls it the "W," though; to locals it is the "Vela" (sail) because of its shape. Open-plan designer rooms have fantastic views and there's a hip, resort feel, with direct beach access and guest DJs at the see-and-be-seen rooftop lounge. There are five restaurants and bars within the hotel itself, but you can also chill out with cocktails, burgers and sand between your toes at the *Salt Beach Club*. €€€€

El Raval

BARCELÓ RAVAL MAP P.54, POCKET MAP B12. Rambla del Raval 17–21. Ⓜ Liceu/Sant Antoni. Ⓦ barcelo.com. Neighbourhood landmark is this glow-in-the-dark tower whose USP is the 360-degree top-floor terrace with plunge pool and city views. Sophisticated, open-plan rooms have a crisp, space-station-style sheen, plus iPhone docks, coffee-makers and other cool comforts, while the slinky lobby "B-lounge" is the place for everything from breakfast to cocktails. €€€

CASA CAMPER MAP P.54, POCKET MAP C11. C/Elisabets 11. Ⓜ Universitat/Liceu. Ⓦ casacamper.com. Synonymous with creative, comfy shoes, Barcelona-based Camper has taken a bold step into the hospitality business with this colourful but minimalist hotel. All the rooms are divided by a corridor: the "sleeping" side faces a six-storey-tall vertical garden; the other part is a "mini-lounge" with a TV, hammock and street-facing balcony. Breakfast and all-day snacks are included. €€€€

HOSTAL CÈNTRIC MAP P.54, POCKET MAP B10. C/Casanova 13. Ⓜ Universitat. Ⓦ hostalcentric.com. A good upper-budget choice a couple of minutes' walk from El Raval proper. The rooms offer plenty of light, plus a/c and private bathrooms. Some include balconies. €€

HOSTAL GRAU MAP P.54, POCKET MAP C10. C/Ramelleres 27. Ⓜ Catalunya. Ⓦ hostalgrau.com. A really friendly *pensión* with attractive, colour-coordinated rooms – superior rooms also have balconies and a touch of modern Catalan style. Two small private apartments in the same building (sleeping two to four, available by the night) offer a bit more independence. €€€

HOTEL ESPAÑA MAP P.54, POCKET MAP C13. C/de Sant Pau 9–11. Ⓜ Liceu. Ⓦ hotelespanya.com. This *modernista* icon has been sumptuously restored, and the gem-like interior – colourful mosaics, sculpted marble, iron swirls and marine motifs – has no equal in Barcelona. Guest rooms are a boutique blend of earth tones and designer style, with rain-showers, iPhone docks and the like, while the handsome house restaurant – known as *Fonda España* – offers contemporary Catalan bistro dishes and is overseen by renowned chef Martín Berasategui. €€€€

HOTEL ONIX LICEO MAP P.54, POCKET MAP B13. C/Nou de la Rambla 36. Ⓜ Liceu/Drassanes. Ⓦ onixhotels.com. Steps from Palau Güell, this four-star hotel features minimalist decor that melds nicely with the building's older architectural elements, such as the grand marble staircase that curves up from the lobby to the second floor. There's a tropical patio and big-for-Barcelona pool on the ground floor and an airy Mozarab-influenced lounge area. €€

HOTEL PENINSULAR MAP P.54, POCKET MAP C13. C/de Sant Pau 34. Ⓜ Liceu. Ⓦ hotelpeninsularbarcelona.com. The interesting old building originally belonged to a priestly order, which explains the slightly cell-like rooms. However, there's nothing spartan about the galleried courtyard (around which the rooms are ranged), hung with tumbling houseplants, while breakfast (included) is served in the arcaded dining room. €€

HOTEL SANT AGUSTÍ MAP P.54, POCKET MAP C12. Pl. Sant Agusti 3. Ⓜ Liceu.

Ⓦ hotelsa.com. Barcelona's oldest hotel occupies a former convent, with front balconies overlooking a restored square and church. It's of three-star standard, with the best rooms located in the attic, from where there are rooftop views. €€€

MARKET HOTEL MAP P.54, POCKET MAP E5. C/Comte Borrell 68, at Ptge. Sant Antoni Abad. Ⓜ Sant Antoni. Ⓦ markethotel.com.es. The designer-budget *Market* makes a splash with its part-Japanese, part-neo-colonial look – think jet-black rooms with hardwood floors and boxy wardrobes topped with travel trunks. €€

Sant Pere

GRAND HOTEL CENTRAL MAP P.65, POCKET MAP E12. Via Laietana 30. Ⓜ Jaume I. Ⓦ grandhotelcentral.com. From the babbling blurb ("it's fresh, it's cool, it's fusion") to the all-in-white rooms with adjustable mood lighting, everything is punchily boutique and in-your-face. Chic, certainly – basic, not at all, though the concept eschews room service, minibars and tonnes of staff at your beck and call. There's a more budget *Chic & Basic* on Carrer dels Tallers (near Plaça Universitat, El Raval) and apartments peppered around the city centre too (details on the website). €€€€

HOTEL CIUTAT BARCELONA MAP P.65, POCKET MAP F13. C/Princesa 33–35 Ⓜ Jaume I. Ⓦ ciutatbarcelona.com. Contemporary comfort at three-star prices in a hotel that's well sited for old-town sightseeing and the Picasso museum.

Accommodation price codes

Throughout this guide we have given a price code to each accommodation review. The codes are based on the cost of a standard double room for one night in peak season. Outside these times rates can drop considerably, sometimes as much as 50 percent, so check establishments' websites and booking sites for the best current rates. Prices do not include breakfast.

€	under €65
€€	€65–€100
€€€	€100–€150
€€€€	over €150

The stylish, colour-coordinated rooms are soundproofed against street noise, if a bit tight on space. Unusually for this price range, there's a cute rooftop bar and small pool for lounging about. €€€

La Ribera

CHIC & BASIC BORN BOUTIQUE MAP P.70, POCKET MAP G13. C/de la Princesa 50. Ⓜ Jaume I. Ⓦ chicandbasic.com. From the babbling blurb ("it's fresh, it's cool, it's fusion") to the all-in-white rooms with adjustable mood lighting, everything is punchily boutique and in-your-face. Chic, certainly – basic, not at all, though the concept eschews room service, minibars and tonnes of staff at your beck and call. There's a more budget *Chic & Basic* on Carrer dels Tallers (near Plaça Universitat, El Raval) and apartments peppered around the city centre too (details on the website). €€

HOSTAL NUEVO COLÓN MAP P.70, POCKET MAP G14. Av. Marquès de l'Argentera 19, 1°. Ⓜ Barceloneta. Ⓦ hostalnuevocolon.es. Run by a friendly family, featuring 24 spacious rooms painted yellow and kitted out with directors' chairs and double glazing. Sunny front rooms all have side views to Ciutadella park, while França station is opposite. €€

Port Olímpic

HOTEL ARTS BARCELONA MAP P.91, POCKET MAP K8. C/Marina 19–21. Ⓜ Ciutadella-Vila Olímpica. Ⓦ hotelartsbarcelona.com. Effortlessly classy rooms feature enormous marble bathrooms and fabulous views. The upper floors belong to *The Club* – an exclusive hotel-within-a-hotel with a luxurious lounge and concierge service. You're only a hop from the beach, but the seafront gardens also have a swimming pool and hot tub. Dining options include the two-Michelin-starred *Enoteca* and the open-air gourmet tapas terrace *Marina Club*. €€€€

Dreta de l'Eixample

CASA BONAY MAP P.96, POCKET MAP G3. Gran Via de Les Corts Catalanes 700. Ⓜ Passeig de Gràcia. Ⓦ casabonay.com. This hotel is set in a neoclassical historical building, with a cosy, hip, eco-friendly interior. After the renovation of the 1896 building the main features – such as the floor tiles – were preserved. The omnipresent potted plants add a lot of charm. Some of the rooms offer private terraces which will give you a secluded place of rest in the centre of the bustling city. €€€€

HOSTAL GIRONA MAP P.96, POCKET MAP G10. C/Girona 24, 1°. Ⓜ Urquinaona. Ⓦ hostalgirona.com. Delightful family-run *pensión* with a wide range of cosy, traditional rooms (some sharing a bathroom, others with a shower or full bath) – the best and biggest have balconies, though you can expect some noise. €€

HOSTAL GOYA MAP P.96, POCKET MAP E10. C/de Pau Claris 74, 1°. Ⓜ Urquinaona. Ⓦ facebook.com/hostalgoyabarcelona. Boutique-style *pensión* that offers stylishly decorated rooms on two floors of a mansion building. There's a fair range of options, with the best rooms opening onto a balcony or terrace. Comfortable sitting areas, and free tea and coffee, are available on both floors. €€€

HOTEL CONDES DE BARCELONA MAP P.96, POCKET MAP H3. Pg. de Gràcia 73–75. Ⓜ Passeig de Gràcia. Ⓦ condesdebarcelona.com. Straddling two sides of C/Mallorca, the *Condes* is fashioned from two former palaces. Its rooms are classily turned out in contemporary style, some with a balcony or private terrace, some with views of Gaudí's La Pedrera. There's a roof terrace with a plunge pool, plus *Alaire*, a hip rooftop cocktail bar. €€€

MANDARIN ORIENTAL MAP P.96, POCKET MAP H3. Pg. de Gràcia 38–40. Ⓜ Passeig de Gràcia. Ⓦ mandarinoriental.com. The sleek *Mandarin Oriental* fills the premises of a former bank building with a soaring white atrium and a selection of extremely thick-walled rooms made from old vaults. The suites are among the finest in Barcelona. There are the obligatory superstar restaurants, *Moments* and *Blanc*, and the super-cool *Banker's Bar*, which has live music and some of the best cocktails in town. €€€€

PRAKTIK BAKERY HOTEL MAP P.96, POCKET MAP H2. C/Provença 279. Ⓜ Diagonal. Ⓦ hotelpraktikbakery.com. Minimalist, all-white designer rooms and a great location aren't the reason for the queue that constantly stretches out of this hotel's door and onto the street. That would be the hotel's bakery run by Baluard, makers of some of Barcelona's best bread. Breakfast doesn't get much better than the buffet of butter croissants, cakes, buns and pastries that await you here each morning. €€€

ROOM-MATE ANNA MAP P.96, POCKET MAP H3. C/d'Aragó 271. Ⓜ Passeig de Gràcia. Ⓦ room-matehotels.com. The Room-Mate chain has cornered the market in affordable mid-range chic and the *Anna* is one of the most stylish, with bright colours and fantastical wallpaper. Reception can provide you with a smartphone that you can use around town and for free international calls. Other perks unusual in this price range include a small rooftop plunge pool. €€€

SAFESTAY PASSEIG DE GRÀCIA MAP P.96, POCKET MAP G3. Pg. de Gràcia 33. Ⓜ Passeig de Gràcia. Ⓦ safestay.com. The biggest hostel in the city occupies a refurbished *modernista* building in a swish midtown location. Private twins, doubles, triples and quads available, all with shower room, balcony and views, while dorms (all en suite) sleep up to fourteen. Excellent facilities include a spectacular roof terrace with views of the famous boulevard. Dorm €, double €€

SIR VICTOR MAP P.96, POCKET MAP H2. C/del Rosselló 265. Ⓜ Diagonal. Ⓦ sirhotels.com. The latest incarnation of the much-mourned *Hotel Omm* is an equally designer affair, with bold colours throughout the generously sized rooms and common areas. There is a quiet spa and well-equipped gym, as well as an excellent restaurant, *Mr Porter*, on the ground floor. The rooftop restaurant is a pleasant enough place during the day, but at night caters to more of a party crowd. €€€€

Sagrada Família and Glòries

URBANY HOSTEL BARCELONA MAP P.106, POCKET MAP M3. Av. Meridiana 97. Ⓜ Clot. Ⓦ urbanyhostels.com. Bumper steel-and-glass 400-bed hostel that's a bit off the beaten track, but on handy metro and airport train routes, and with amazing views of Torre Glòries. The rooms are like space-shuttle pods – boxy en-suites with pull-down beds (sleeping two to eight), power-showers and key-card lockers – that are just as viable for couples on a budget as backpackers (there are also private rooms). There's a bar and terrace, plus free gym, jacuzzi and pool entry in the same building. Dorm €, single/twin €€

HOTEL EUROSTARS MONUMENTAL MAP P.106, POCKET MAP K3. C/Consell de Cent 498–500. Ⓜ Monumental. Ⓦ eurostars hotels.com. An excellent-value four-star choice within walking distance of the Sagrada Família. The 45 rooms are crisply appointed in dark wood and earth tones, staff are really helpful and the top-floor suites have terrace views of the Gaudí church. €€€

Esquerra de l'Eixample

ALTERNATIVE CREATIVE YOUTH HOME MAP P.114, POCKET MAP G4. Ronda Universitat 17. Ⓜ Universitat/Catalunya. Ⓦ alternative-barcelona.com. The hostel hangout for an art crowd who love the laidback vibe, projection lounge, cool music and city-savvy staff. The regular hostel stuff is well designed too, with a walk-in kitchen and a maximum of 24 people spread across three small dorms. €

MIDMOST HOTEL BARCELONA MAP P.114, POCKET MAP C10. C/Pelai 14. Ⓜ Universitat. Ⓦ hotelmidmost.com. The boutique little three-star sister to the Dreta's *Hotel Majestic* has harmoniously toned rooms and snazzy bathrooms. Space is at a premium, but some rooms have cute private terraces, others street-side balconies, while best of all are the romantic roof terrace and pool. €€€€

NOBU HOTEL MAP P.114, POCKET MAP C2. Av. Roma 2–4. Ⓜ Sants Estació. Ⓦ barcelona.nobuhotels.com. The landmark five-star deluxe hotel outside Sants station features sweeping views from all sides. Breakfast on the 23rd floor is a buzz; there's also a spa with indoor pool, and two superb Japanese restaurants, as you would expect from masterchef Nobu. €€€€

HOTEL PRAKTIK RAMBLA MAP P.114, POCKET MAP G4. Rambla de Catalunya 27. Ⓜ Passeig de Gràcia. Ⓦ hotelpraktikrambla.com. This new boutique hotel in a converted *modernista* mansion keeps the design touches toned down and lets the architecture do the talking. Big, high-ceilinged rooms (especially the deluxe doubles), look out onto a tranquil terrace, complete with burbling fountain, where you can enjoy the sunshine in peace. €€€

SOHO HOTEL MAP P.114, POCKET MAP G4. Gran Via de les Corts Catalanes 543–545. Ⓜ Urgell. Ⓦ hotelsohobarcelona.com. A smart, modern and no-nonsense hotel, not quite in the thick of things, but a stone's throw away from public transit. There is a small rooftop pool on a wood-decked terrace with superb views. €€€

SOMNIO BARCELONA MAP P.114, POCKET MAP G4. C/Diputació 251 2°. Ⓜ Passeig de Gràcia. Ⓦ somniohostels.com. Sisters Lauren and Lee from Chicago bring their passion for Barcelona right into their upscale *pensión*, dropping "tips for the day" into your room each morning. Simple but smart rooms with wood-block floors cater for singles, couples and friends. There are four spacious twin rooms, four double rooms (two en suite) and a single. Some have balconies. €€€

Gràcia

BARCELONA XANASCAT MAP P.122. Pg. de la Mare de Déu del Coll 41–51. Ⓜ Vallcarca. Ⓦ xanascat.cat. A popular hostel, set in a beautifully converted mansion with gardens, terrace and great city views, with dorms sleeping six, eight or twelve. It's a long way from the centre,

though it's close to Park Güell and the transport links are good – just a short walk to the metro, or buses (#V17 from Plaça d'Urquinaona, plus night buses) stop just across the street. €

CASA GRÀCIA MAP P.121, POCKET MAP H2. Pg. de Gràcia 116. Ⓜ Diagonal. Ⓦ casagraciabcn.com. A vibrant and stylish space spread over six floors in a *modernista* building, with bonuses like a concierge, themed dinners and evening concerts. The rooms (from dorms to doubles to six-bed private rooms) have a/c and are en suite, while the deluxe suite pampers with a spa bath, slippers and bathrobes. Though *Casa Gracia* is technically a hostel, you'll feel like you're staying in a (pretty good) hotel. €€

GENERATOR BARCELONA MAP P.121, POCKET MAP H2. C/de Corsega 373. Ⓜ Diagonal. Ⓦ generatorhostels.com. Big, bright and abuzz with people having fun, the *Generator* lounge frequently features live music, DJ sets and art performances, as well as a pool table and large-screen TV. Rooms are clean and modern, and there's 24-hour reception. €

HOTEL CASA FUSTER MAP P.121, POCKET MAP H1. Pg. de Gràcia 132. Ⓜ Diagonal. Ⓦ hotelcasafuster.com. *Modernista* architect Lluís Domènech i Montaner's magnificent Casa Fuster (1908) is the backdrop for five-star deluxe luxury with service to match. Rooms are in earth tones, with huge beds, smart bathrooms, and remote-controlled light and heat, while public areas make full use of the architectural heritage – from the magnificent pillared lobby bar, the *Café Vienés*, to the panoramic roof terrace and pool. There's also a contemporary restaurant, *Aleia*, plus fitness centre, sauna and 24hr room service. €€€€

Montjuïc

HOTEL MIRAMAR MAP P.81, POCKET MAP E7. Pl. Carlos Ibañez 3. Ⓜ Paral. lel and Funicular de Montjuïc. Ⓦ hotelmiramarbarcelona.com. The remodelled *Miramar* has 75 stylish rooms with sweeping views over the city. From the architecture books in the lounge to the terrace jacuzzis, you're in designer heaven, augmented by a stunning pool and tranquil gardens. €€€€

Tibidabo

GRAN HOTEL LA FLORIDA MAP P.137. Carretera Vallvidrera a Tibidabo 83–93, 7km from the centre. Ⓦ hotellaflorida.com. This five-star place on Tibidabo mountain re-creates the glory days of the 1950s, when *La Florida* was at the centre of Barcelona high society. Its terraces and pools have amazing views, while some of the seventy rooms and suites have private gardens or terraces and jacuzzis. Jazz sessions in the club are not to be missed. There's also a spa, restaurant, poolside bar and shuttle-bus service to town. €€€€

ACCOMMODATION

ESSENTIALS

Montjuïc cable car

Arrival

In most cases, you can be off the plane, train or bus and in your central Barcelona hotel room within the hour. Note that arrivals at the airports at Girona (90km north of the city) or Reus (110km south) do have reliable connecting bus and train services, but will mean up to a 90-minute journey to Barcelona city centre.

By air

Barcelona's airport (Josep Tarradellas Barcelona-El Prat, ⓦ aena.es) is 18km southwest of the city. A **taxi** to the centre costs up to €40, including the airport surcharge (plus other surcharges for travel after 8pm or at weekends). Far cheaper is the **airport train** (6.08am–11.38pm; 19min; €4.60; ⓦ rodalies.gencat.cat), which runs every thirty minutes to Barcelona Sants station (see "By train") and then continues on to Passeig de Gràcia (best stop for Eixample, Plaça de Catalunya and La Rambla). It departs from Terminal T2, and there's a free shuttle bus to the station from T1 which takes around ten minutes. The Barcelona Card (available at the airport) and city travel passes are valid on the airport train.

Alternatively, the **Aerobús** service (Mon–Sat 5.30am–1am; 30min; €6.75 or €11.65 return, departures every 5–10min from T1 and T2; ⓦ aerobusbcn.com) stops in the city at Plaça d'Espanya, Gran Via–Urgell, Plaça Universitat and Plaça de Catalunya. Aerobús departures back to the airport leave from in front of El Corte Inglés in Plaça de Catalunya – note that there are separate services to terminals T1 and T2.

By bus

The main bus terminal is the **Estació del Nord** (ⓦ barcelonanord.

barcelona; ⓂArc de Triomf) on C/ Ali-Bei, three blocks north of Parc de la Ciutadella. Various companies operate services across Catalunya, Spain and Europe from here – it's a good idea to reserve a ticket in advance on long-distance routes (a day before at the station is usually fine, or buy online). Some intercity and international services also make a stop at the bus terminal behind Barcelona Sants station. Either way, you're only a short metro ride from the city centre.

By train

The national rail service is operated by RENFE (ⓦ renfe.com). The city's main station is **Barcelona Sants**, 3km west of the centre, with a metro station (ⓂSants Estació) that links directly to La Rambla (ⓂLiceu), Plaça de Catalunya and Passeig de Gràcia. The high-speed AVE line between Barcelona and Madrid has cut the fastest journey between the cities to under three hours. These services also arrive at and depart from Barcelona Sants, though a second high-speed station is under construction in the north of the city.

Some Spanish intercity services and international trains also stop at **Estació de França**, 1km east of La Rambla and close to ⓂBarceloneta.

Regional and local commuter train services are operated by Renfe (ⓦ renfe.com) and Ferrocarrils de la Generalitat de Catalunya, or **FGC** (ⓦ fgc.cat), with the main stations at **Plaça de Catalunya**, at the top of La Rambla (for trains from coastal towns north of the city); **Plaça d'Espanya** (for Montserrat); and **Passeig de Gràcia** (Catalunya provincial destinations).

Getting around

Barcelona has an excellent integrated transport system which comprises the metro, buses, trams and local trains, plus a network of funiculars and cable cars. The local transport authority has a useful website (🌐 tmb.cat, English-language version available) with full timetable and ticket information, while a city transport map and information is posted at major bus stops and all metro and tram stations.

The metro

The quickest way of getting around Barcelona is by **metro**, which runs on eight main lines.

There's a limited network of stations in the Old Town, but you can take the metro directly to La Rambla (Catalunya, Liceu or Drassanes), and to the edge of the Barri Gòtic, El Raval and La Ribera.

Metro entrances are marked with a red diamond sign with an "M". Its **hours of operation** are Monday to Thursday, plus Sunday and public holidays 5am to midnight; Friday 5am to 2am; Saturday and the day before a public holiday, 24hr service. The system is safe, but beware of pickpockets.

Tickets and travel passes

On all the city's public transport (including night buses and funiculars), you can buy a **single ticket** every time you ride (€2.40, or €5.15 to or from the airport), but it's much cheaper to buy a **targeta** – a discount ticket card. They are available at metro, train and tram stations, but not on the buses.

Best general ticket deal is the T-casual ("tay caz-oo-al" in Catalan) *targeta* (€11.35), valid for ten journeys, with changes between methods of transport allowed within 75 minutes. This card (also available at newsagents' kiosks and government tobacco shops) is valid until the next fare increase (generally the end of January in the year after purchase).

Other useful *targetes* include the multiday combos (Hola Barcelona) for up to five days (€38.20). Prices given are for passes valid as far as the Zone 1 city limits, which in practice is everywhere you're likely to want to go except Montserrat and Sitges. For trips to these and other out-of-town destinations, buy a specific ticket.

Trams

The **tram** system (🌐 tram.cat) runs on six lines, with departures every eight to twenty minutes throughout the day from 5am to midnight. Lines **T1, T2 and T3** depart from Plaça Francesc Macià and run along the uptown part of Avinguda Diagonal to suburban destinations in the northwest – useful tourist stops are at L'Illa shopping and the Maria Cristina and Palau Reial metro stations. **Line T4** operates from Ciutadella-Vila Olímpica (where there's also a metro station) and runs up past the zoo and TNC (the National Theatre) to Glòries, before running down the lower part of Avinguda Diagonal to Diagonal Mar and the Fòrum site. You're unlikely to use the more suburban lines T5 and T6.

Emergency numbers

Call ☏ 112 for emergency ambulance, police and fire services; for the national police service call ☏ 091.

Buses

Most **buses** operate daily, roughly from 4am or 5am until 10.30pm, though some lines stop earlier and some run on until after midnight. Night bus services fill in the gaps on all the main routes, with services every twenty to 60 minutes from around 10pm to 4am. Many bus routes (including all night buses) stop in or near Plaça de Catalunya, but the full route is marked at each bus stop, along with a timetable.

City tours

The number of tours available is bewildering, and you can see the sights on anything from a Segway to a hot-air balloon. A good place to start is the official Barcelona Turisme website (ⓦbarcelonaturisme.com), which has a dedicated tours section offering online sales and discounts.

Highest profile are the two tour-bus operators with daily board-at-will, open-top services (one day €33, two days €40), which drop you outside every attraction in the city. The choice is between **Barcelona City Tour** (ⓦbarcelonatours.es) or the **Bus Turístic** (ⓦbarcelonabusturistic.cat), with frequent departures from Plaça de Catalunya and many other stops – tickets are available on board. Both services provide discount vouchers for assorted sights, restaurants and shops.

Advance booking is advised (at Pl. de Catalunya tourist office) for **Barcelona Walking Tours**' (ⓦbarcelonaturisme.com) two-hour historical Barri Gòtic tour (daily all year, in English at 9.30am). There are also "Picasso", "*Modernisme*" and "Gourmet" walking tours, among others.

Long-time resident Nick Lloyd's **Spanish Civil War** tours (ⓦthespanishcivilwar.com) weave human stories with the historical events that shaped the city. Delivered in English, these absorbing half-day tours include a coffee break. Nick

also runs occasional tours themed around 'green Montjuïc', the history of anarchism in Barcelona, and privately booked tours on Orwell's Barcelona.

Devour Tours (ⓦdevourtours.com) as a range of food tours around the city led by passionate guides.

There are flyers and **bike tour** outfits everywhere, with follow-the-leader cycle packs riding through the Old Town alleys on guided 3hr tours.

At any time of year, the sparkling harbour waters invite a cruise and **Las Golondrinas** (ⓦlasgolondrinas.com) daily sightseeing boats depart (at least hourly June–Sept, less frequently Oct–May) from the quayside opposite the Columbus statue, at the bottom of La Rambla (ⓦDrassanes). Two of the services visit either the port (40min) or port and local coast (1hr).

There are also catamaran trips around the port with **Catamaran Orsom** (ⓦbarcelona-orsom.com). These include sunset jazz cruises, a midday cruise and a chill-out cruise.

Cycling and bike rental

The city council is investing heavily in cycle lanes and bike schemes, notably the **Bicing** pick-up and drop-off scheme (ⓦbicing.cat). You'll see the red bikes and bike stations all over the city, but Bicing is not available to tourists, only to locals who are encouraged to use the bikes for short trips. To rent a bike you need to be registered as a Barcelona resident.

There are plenty of other **bike rental** outfits aimed at tourists. Rental costs from around €15 a day with companies all over town, including Donkey Republic (ⓦdonkey.bike) and Bike Rental Barcelona (ⓦbikerentalbarcelona.com).

Currently there are around 270km of **cycle paths** throughout the city, with plans to double the network in the future. Not all locals have embraced the bike yet, and some cycle paths are still ignored by cars or clogged with pedestrians, indignantly reluctant to give way to two-wheelers. But on the whole, cycling around Barcelona is not the completely hairy experience it was just a few years ago, while you can always get **off-road** in the Parc de Collserola, where there are waymarked trails through the woods and hills.

Funiculars and cable cars

As well as the regular city options, Barcelona also has some fun transport trips and historic survivors. There are **funicular railways** up to Montjuïc and Tibidabo, while summer and year-round weekend visits to Tibidabo also combine a funicular trip with a ride on the clanking antique tram, the **Tramvia Blau**. Best of all, though, are the two **cable car** (*telefèric*) rides: from Barceloneta across the harbour to Montjuïc, and then from the top station of the Montjuïc funicular right the way up to the castle.

Taxis

There are taxi ranks outside major train and metro stations, in main squares, near large hotels and at places along the main avenues.

To book a taxi in advance you can call them up – though few of the operators speak English, and you'll be charged an extra €4 or €5) – or reserve through their website or app, often available in English try: Barnataxi (⊚ barnataxi.com, ☎ 933 222 222); Radio Taxi (⊚ radiotaxi033. com, ☎ 936 936 936); or for people with reduced mobility, Taxi Amic (⊚ taxiamic.cat, ☎ 934 208 088).

Trains

The FGC **commuter train line** has its main stations at Plaça de Catalunya and Plaça d'Espanya, used when going to Sarrià, Vallvidrera, Tibidabo and Montserrat. The national rail service, RENFE (⊚ renfe.com), runs all the other services out of Barcelona, with local lines designated as **Rodalies/Cercanías**. The hub is Barcelona Sants station, with services also passing through Plaça de Catalunya (heading west), Passeig de Gràcia (south) and Estació de França (north). Arrive in plenty of time to buy a ticket, as queues are often long, though for most regional destinations you can use the automatic vending machines instead.

Directory A–Z

Accessible travel

Barcelona's airport and Aerobús are fully accessible to travellers in wheelchairs. Almost all metro stations are now accessible – see ⊚ tmb. cat/en/transport-accessible for full details. City buses have all been adapted for wheelchair use, while the city information line – ☎ 010 – has accessibility information for museums, galleries, hotels, restaurants, museums, bars and stores. Be warned that some Old Town attractions have steps, cobbles or other impediments to access.

Addresses

The main address abbreviations are Av. (for Avinguda, avenue), C/ (Carrer, street), Pg. (Passeig, boulevard/street), Bxda. (Baixada, alley), Ptge. (Passatge, passage) and Pl. (Plaça, square). The address "C/Picasso 2, 4°" means: Picasso Street, number two, fourth floor.

Crime

Take all the usual precautions and be on guard when on public transport or on the crowded Rambla and the medieval streets to either side. Easiest place to report a crime is the

Gùardia Urbana (municipal police) for each district (☎092, ⊕bcn.cat/guardiaurbana; 24hr, English spoken). For a police report for your insurance go to C/Nou de la Rambla 80, El Raval (Ⓜ Paral·lel, English-speaking line ☎933 062 300, inside Spain ☎092).

Electricity

The electricity supply is 220v and plugs come with two round pins – bring an adapter (and transformer, if necessary) to use chargers for UK and US mobile phones, cameras, etc.

Embassies and consulates

Australia, Av. Diagonal 433, Eixample, Ⓜ Diagonal, ☎937 155 866, ⊕spain.embassy.gov.au; UK, Av. Diagonal 477, Eixample, Ⓜ Hospital Clínic, ☎933 666 200, ⊕ukinspain.fco.gov.uk; Canada, Pl. Catalunya 9, Ⓜ Catalunya, ☎932 703 614, ⊕canadainternational.gc.ca; Republic of Ireland, Gran Via Carlos III 94, Les Corts, Ⓜ Maria Cristina/Les Corts, ☎934 915 021, ⊕dfa.ie; New Zealand, Trav. de Gràcia 64, Gràcia, FGC Gràcia, ☎932 095 048, ⊕/bit.ly/NZConsulate; USA, Pg. de la Reina Elisenda 23, Sarrià, FGC Reina Elisenda, ☎932 802 227, ⊕usembassy.gov.

Health

The following central hospitals have 24hr accident and emergency services: Centre Perecamps, Av. Drassanes 13–15, El Raval, Ⓜ Drassanes, ☎934 410 600; Hospital Clínic i Provincial, C/Villaroel 170, Eixample, Ⓜ Hospital Clínic, ☎932 275 400. EU (and UK) citizens receive free or reduced cost treatment if they bring their EHIC (or GHIC) card and passport.

Usual pharmacy hours are 9am to 1pm and 4 to 8pm. At least one in each neighbourhood is open 24hr (and marked as such).

LGBTQ+ travellers

Epicentre of the gay scene is the so-called Gaixample, an area of a few blocks near the university in the Esquerra de l'Eixample. The annual Pride festival runs for ten days in June (⊕pridebarcelona.org). General listings magazine *Time Out Barcelona* can put you on the right track for bars and clubs. For other information, contact the lesbian and gay cultural centre Casal Lambda (⊕lambda.cat).

Lost property

Anything recovered by police, or left on public transport, is sent to the Oficina de Troballes (municipal lost property office) at C/Ciutat, Barri Gòtic, Ⓜ Jaume, I/Catalunya (Mon–Fri 9am–2pm; ☎010). You could also try the transport office at Ⓜ Universitat.

Money

Spain's currency is the euro (€), with notes issued in denominations of 5, 10, 20, 50, 100, 200 and 500 euros, and coins in denominations of 1, 2, 5, 10, 20 and 50 cents, and 1 and 2 euros. Normal banking hours are Monday to Friday from 8.30am to 2pm, and there

Eating out price codes

The price codes used throughout this guide are as follows, and generally refer to two courses, plus one drink and service, for one person:

€	under €25
€€	€25–45
€€€	€45–75
€€€€	over €75

are out-of-hours exchange offices down La Rambla, as well as at the airport, Barcelona Sants station and the Pl. de Catalunya tourist office. ATMs are available all over the city, and you can usually withdraw up to €300 a day.

Museums and passes

Many museums and galleries offer free admission on the first or last Sunday of the month, and most museums are free on the saints' days of February 12, April 23 and September 24, plus May 18 (International Museum Day). The useful Barcelona Card (3, 4 or 5 days; ⓦ barcelonacard.org) offers free public transport, plus museum and attraction discounts. The Articket (three months; ⓦ articketbcn.org) covers free admission into six major art galleries, while the *Ruta del Modernisme* (one year; ⓦ rutadelmodernisme.com) is an excellent English-language guidebook and discount-voucher package that covers 116 *modernista* buildings, plus other benefits.

Opening hours

Basic working hours are Monday to Saturday 9.30 or 10am to 1.30pm and 4.30 to 8 or 9pm, though many offices and shops don't open on Saturday afternoons. Local cafés, bars and markets open from around 8am, while shopping centres, major stores and large supermarkets tend to open all day from 10am to 9pm, with some even open on Sunday. Museums and galleries often have restricted Sunday and public holiday hours, while on Mondays most are closed all day.

Phones

The cheapest way to make an international call is to go to a *locutorio* (phone centre); these are scattered throughout the old city, particularly in the Raval and Ribera. You'll be assigned a cabin to make your calls, and afterwards you pay in cash. Before you travel, check with your contract provider if your mobile phone will work in Spain, and whether you can use your data and calls on a roaming deal, or purchase a deal to allow you to do so.

Post

The main post office (Correus) is on Pl. de Correus, at the eastern end of Pg. de Colom, in the Barri Gòtic (Mon–Fri 8.30am–9.30pm, Sat 8.30am–2pm; ⓜ Barceloneta/Jaume I). For stamps it's easier to visit a tobacconist (look for the brown-and-yellow *tabac* sign), found on virtually every street.

Public holidays

Official holidays are: Jan 1 (Cap d'Any, New Year's Day); Jan 6 (Epifanía, Epiphany); Good Friday & Easter Monday; May 1 (Dia del Treball, May Day/ Labour Day); June 24 (Dia de Sant Joan, St John's Day); Aug 15 (L'Assumpció, Assumption of the Virgin); Sept 11 (Diada Nacional, Catalan National Day); Sept 24 (Festa de la Mercè, Our Lady of Mercy, Barcelona's patron saint); Oct 12 (Dia de la Hispanidad, Spanish National Day); Nov 1 (Tots Sants, All Saints' Day); Dec 6 (Dia de la Constitució, Constitution Day); Dec 8 (La Immaculada, Immaculate Conception); Dec 25 (Nadal, Christmas Day); Dec 26 (Sant Esteve, St Stephen's Day).

Tickets

You can buy concert, sporting and exhibition tickets through Ticketea (ⓦ ticketea.com), Eventbrite (ⓦ eventbrite.es) and Ticketmaster (ⓦ ticketmaster.es). For advance tickets for all city council (Ajuntament) sponsored concerts visit the Palau de la Virreina, Rambla 99.

Time

Barcelona is one hour ahead of the UK, six hours ahead of New York and Toronto, nine hours ahead of Los Angeles, nine hours behind Sydney and eleven hours behind Auckland. This applies except for brief periods during the change-overs to and from daylight saving (in Spain the clocks go forward in the last week in March, back again in the last week of Oct).

Tipping

Locals leave only a few cents or round up the change for a coffee or drink, and a euro or two for most meals, though fancier restaurants will expect ten to fifteen percent. Taxi drivers normally get around five percent.

Tourist information

The city's tourist board, Turisme de Barcelona (☎ 932 853 834, ⓦ barcelonaturisme.com), has its main office in Plaça de Catalunya (daily 8.30am–8.30pm; Ⓜ Catalunya), down the steps in the southeast corner of the square, where there's a tours service and accommodation desk. There's also an office in the Barri Gòtic at Plaça de Sant Jaume, entrance at C/Ciutat 2 (Mon–Sat 10am–8pm; Ⓜ Jaume I), and staffed information booths dotted across the city. The city's ☎ 010 telephone enquiries service (available 24hr; some English-speaking staff available) can help with questions about transport, public services and other matters. The city hall (Ajuntament; ⓦ bcn.cat) and regional government (Generalitat; ⓦ gencat.cat) websites are also mines of information about every aspect of cultural, social and working life in Barcelona. Concerts, exhibitions and festivals are covered in full at the walk-in office of the Institut de Cultura at the Palau de la Virreina, La Rambla 99, Ⓜ Liceu (ⓦ bcn.cat/cultura; daily 10am–8.30pm).

Travelling with children

Taking your children to Barcelona doesn't pose insurmountable travel problems. There's plenty to do, whether it's a day at the beach or a daredevil cable-car ride, while if you coincide with one of Barcelona's festivals, you'll be able to join in with the local celebrations, from sweet-tossing and puppet shows to fireworks and human castles. For ideas, check out the English-language site ⓦ barcelonacolours.com, which is packed with information on fun activities, child-friendly restaurants and so on. Most establishments are baby-friendly in the sense that you'll be made very welcome if you turn up with a child in tow. Many museum cloakrooms, for example, will be happy to look after your pushchair as you carry your child around the building, while restaurants will make a fuss of your little one. However, specific facilities are not as widespread as they are in the UK or US. Baby-changing areas are relatively rare, except in department stores and shopping centres, and even where they do exist they are not always up to scratch. By far the best is at El Corte Inglés, though most major shopping centres now have pull-down changing tables in their public toilets. Local restaurants tend not to offer children's menus (though they will try to accommodate specific requests), highchairs are not always provided and restaurants open relatively late for lunch and dinner. Despite best intentions, you might find yourself eating in one of the international franchise restaurants, which tend to be open throughout the day. You'll pay from around €25–30/hr for babysitting if arranged through your hotel; or contact Barcelona Babysitter (€25/hr; enquiries Mon–Sat 9am–9pm; ⓦ bcnbabysitter.com), who can provide English-speaking nannies and babysitters.

Water

Water from the tap is safe to drink, but generally doesn't taste very nice. You'll be given bottled mineral water in a bar or restaurant.

Festivals and events

Almost any month you visit Barcelona you'll coincide with a festival, event or holiday. The best are picked out below, but for a full list check out the Ajuntament (city hall) website Ⓦ bcn. cat/cultura.

Festes de Santa Eulàlia

Mid-February
Ⓦ **bcn.cat/santaeulalia**
Winter festival around February 12 in honour of the young Barcelona girl who suffered a beastly martyrdom at the hands of the Romans. There are parades, concerts, fireworks and *sardana* dancing.

Carnaval/Carnestoltes

Week before Lent (Feb or March)
Costumed parades and other carnival events across every city neighbourhood. Sitges, down the coast, has the most outrageous celebrations.

Dia de Sant Jordi

April 23
St George's Day celebrates Catalunya's patron saint, with hundreds of book and flower stalls down La Rambla and elsewhere.

Primavera Sound

Usually late May
Ⓦ **primaverasound.com**
The city's hottest music festival attracts top names in the rock, indie and electronica world.

Sónar

June Ⓦ **sonar.es**
Europe's biggest, most cutting-edge electronic music, multimedia and urban art festival presents three days of brilliant noise and spectacle.

Verbena/Dia de Sant Joan

June 23/24
The "eve" and "day" of St John herald a "night of fire", involving bonfires and fireworks (particularly on Montjuïc) and watching the sun come up on the beach.

Festival de Barcelona Grec

From end June to August
Ⓦ **grec.bcn.cat**
This is the city's main performing arts festival, with many events staged at Montjuïc's Teatre Grec.

Festes de la Mercè

End September Ⓦ **bcn.cat/merce**
The city's main festival is celebrated for a week around September 24, with costumed giants, firework displays and human tower competitions.

Festival Internacional de Jazz

October/November
Ⓦ **jazz.barcelona**
The annual jazz festival attracts big-name artists to the clubs, as well as smaller-scale street concerts.

FESTIVALS AND EVENTS

Celebrating Catalan-style

Central to any traditional Barcelona festival is the parade of *gegants*, five-metre-high giants with papier-mâché or fibreglass heads. Also typically Catalan is the *correfoc* ("fire-running"), where drummers, dragons and demons cavort in the streets. Meanwhile, teams of *castellers* – "castle-makers" – pile person upon person to see who can construct the highest tower.

Chronology

c230 BC Carthaginians found the settlement of "Barcino", probably on the heights of Montjuïc.

218–201 BC Romans expel Carthaginians from Iberian peninsula in Second Punic War. Roman Barcino is established around today's Barri Gòtic.

304 AD Santa Eulàlia – one of the city's two patron saints – is martyred by Romans for refusing to renounce Christianity.

c350 AD Roman city walls are built, as threat of invasion grows.

415 Visigoths sweep across Spain and establish temporary capital in Barcino (later "Barcelona").

711 Moorish conquest of Spain. Barcelona eventually forced to surrender (719).

801 Barcelona retaken by Louis the Pious, son of Charlemagne. Frankish counties of Catalunya become a buffer zone, known as the Spanish Marches.

878 Guifré el Pelós (Wilfred the Hairy) declared first Count of Barcelona, founding a dynastic line that was to rule until 1410.

985 Moorish sacking of city. Sant Pau del Camp – the city's oldest surviving church – built after this date.

1137 Dynastic union of Catalunya and Aragón established.

1213–76 Reign of Jaume I, "the Conqueror", expansion of empire and beginning of Catalan golden age.

1282–1387 Barcelona at the centre of an aggressively mercantile Mediterranean empire. Successive rulers construct most of Barcelona's best-known Gothic buildings.

1348 The Black Death strikes, killing half of Barcelona's population.

1391 Pogrom against the city's Jewish population.

1410 Death of Martí el Humà (Martin the Humane), last of Catalan count-kings. Beginning of the end of Catalan influence in the Mediterranean.

1469 Marriage of Ferdinand of Aragón and Isabel of Castile.

1479 Ferdinand succeeds to Catalan-Aragón crown, and Catalunya's fortunes decline. Inquisition introduced to Barcelona, leading to forced flight of the Jews.

1493 Christopher Columbus received in Barcelona after his triumphant return from New World. The shifting of trade routes away from the Mediterranean and across the Atlantic further impoverishes the city.

1516 Spanish crown passes to Habsburgs and Madrid is established as capital of Spanish empire.

1640–52 The uprising known as the "Wars of the Reapers" declares Catalunya an independent republic. Barcelona is besieged and eventually surrenders to the Spanish army.

1714 After War of Spanish Succession, throne passes to Bourbons. Barcelona subdued on September 11 (now Catalan National Day); Ciutadella fortress built, Catalan language banned and parliament abolished.

1755 Barceloneta district laid out – gridded layout is an early example of urban planning.

1778 Steady increase in trade; Barcelona's economy improves.

1814 After Peninsular War (1808–14), French finally driven out, with Barcelona the last city to fall.

1859 Old city walls demolished and Eixample district built to accommodate growing population.

1882 Work begins on Sagrada Família; Antoni Gaudí takes charge two years later.

1888 Universal Exhibition held at Parc de la Ciutadella. Modernista architects start to make their mark.

1893 First stirrings of anarchist unrest. Liceu opera house bombed.

1901 Pablo Picasso's first public exhibition held at *Els Quatre Gats* tavern.

1909 Setmana Tràgica (Tragic Week) of rioting. Many churches destroyed.

1922 Park Güell opens to the public.

1926 Antoni Gaudí is run over by a tram; Barcelona stops en masse for his funeral.

1929 International Exhibition held at Montjuïc.

1936–39 Spanish Civil War. Barcelona at the heart of Republican cause, with George Orwell and other volunteers arriving to fight. City eventually falls to Nationalists on January 26, 1939.

1939–75 Spain under Franco. Generalitat president Lluís Companys executed and Catalan language banned. Emigration encouraged from south to dilute Catalan identity. Franco dies in 1975.

1977 First democratic Spanish elections for 40 years.

1978–80 Generalitat re-established and Statute of Autonomy approved. Conservative nationalist government elected.

1992 Olympics held in Barcelona. Rebuilding projects transform Montjuïc and the waterfront.

1995 MACBA (contemporary art museum) opens, and signals the regeneration of El Raval district.

2006 New Statute of Autonomy agreed with Spain.

2014 Constitutional Court of Spain deems the Catalan government's 2013 declaration of sovereignty to be unconstitutional.

2017 On 17 August 2017 in a jihadist attack, a man drove a van into the crowd of pedestrians on La Rambla, killing 13 people and injuring 130.

2017 In a referendum deemed illegal and violently suppressed by the Spanish government, Catalans vote in favour of the region becoming an independent state. The Catalan parliament declares independence, but is promptly dissolved by the Spanish government, which then calls for new regional elections, won again by pro-independence parties.

2023 After a general election in which no party commanded a majority vote – in part due to the support of Catalan and Basque nationalists – the formation of a new government looked to drag on into 2024.

Catalan

In Barcelona, Catalan (català) has more or less taken over from Castilian (castellano) Spanish as the language on street signs and maps. On paper it looks like a cross between French and Spanish and is generally easy to read if you know those two. Few visitors realize how important Catalan is to those who speak it: never commit the error of calling it a dialect. Despite the preponderance of the Catalan language you'll get by perfectly well in Spanish as long as you're aware of the use of Catalan in timetables, on menus, and so on. However, you'll generally get a good reception if you at least try communicating in the local language.

Pronunciation

Don't be tempted to use the few rules of Spanish pronunciation you may know – in particular the soft Spanish Z and C don't apply, so unlike in the rest of Spain, the city is not Barthelona but Barcelona, as in English.

a as in hat if stressed, as in alone when unstressed.

e varies, but usually as in get.

i as in police.

ig sounds like the "tch" in the English scratch; lleig (ugly) is pronounced "yeah-tch".

o a round, full sound, when stressed, otherwise like a soft U sound.

u somewhere between the U of put and rule.

ç sounds like an English S; plaça is pronounced "plassa".

c followed by an E or I is soft; otherwise hard.

g followed by E or I is like the "zh" in Zhivago; otherwise hard.

h is always silent.

j as in the French "Jean".

l.l is best pronounced (for foreigners) as a single L sound; but for Catalan speakers it has two distinct L sounds.

ll sounds like an English Y or LY, like the "yuh" sound in million.

n as in English, though before F or V it sometimes sounds like an M.

ny corresponds to the Castilian Ñ.

qu before E or I sounds like K; before A or O, or if the U has an umlaut (Ü), sounds like KWE, as in quit.

r is rolled, but only at the start of a word; at the end it's often silent.

t is pronounced as in English, though sometimes it sounds like a D; as in viatge or dotze.

v at the start of a word sounds like B; in all other positions it's a soft F sound.

w is pronounced like a B/V.

x is like SH or CH in most words, though in some, like exit, it sounds like an X.

z is like the English Z in zoo.

Words and phrases

Basics

Yes, No, OK Sí, No, Val
Please, Thank you Si us plau, Gràcies
Hello, Goodbye Hola, Adéu
Good morning Bon dia
Good afternoon/night Bona tarde/nit
See you later Fins després
Sorry Ho sento
Excuse me Perdoni
I (don't) understand (No) Ho entenc
Do you speak English? Parleu anglès?
Where? When? On? Quan?
What? How much? Què? Quant?
Here, There Aquí, Allí/Allá
This, That Això, Allò
Open, Closed Obert, Tancat
With, Without Amb, Sense
Good, Bad Bo(na), Dolent(a)
Big, Small Gran, Petit(a)
Cheap, Expensive Barat(a), Car(a)
I want Vull (pronounced "vwee")
I'd like Voldria
Do you know? Vostès saben?
I don't know No sé
There is (Is there?) Hi ha(?)
What's that? Què és això?
Do you have...? Té...?
Today, Tomorrow Avui, Demà

Accommodation

Do you have a room? Té alguna habitació?

...with two beds/double bed ...amb dos llits/ llit per dues persones

...with shower/bath ...amb dutxa/bany

It's for one person (two people) Per a una persona (dues persones)

For one night (one week) Per una nit (una setmana)

It's fine, how much is it? Esta bé, quant és?

Don't you have anything cheaper? En té de més bonpreu?

Directions and transport

How do I get to...? Per anar a...?

Left, Right A l'esquerra, A la dreta

Straight on Tot recte

Where is...? On és...?

...the bus station ...l'estació de autobuses

...the train station ...l'estació

...the nearest bank ...el banc més a prop

...the post office ...l'oficina de correus

...the toilet ...el bany

Where does the bus De on surt el

to...leave from? autobús a...?

Is this the train for Aquest tren va a

Barcelona? Barcelona?

I'd like a (return) ticket to... Voldria un bitlet (d'anar i tornar) a...

What time does it leave (arrive in)? A quina hora surt (arriba a)?

Days of the week

Monday dilluns

Tuesday dimarts

Wednesday dimecres

Thursday dijous

Friday divendres

Saturday dissabte

Sunday diumenge

Months of the Year

January Gener

February Febrer

March Març

April Abril

May Maig

June Juny

July Juliol

August Agost

September Setembre

October Octobre

November Novembre

December Desembre

Numbers

1 un(a)

2 dos (dues)

3 tres

4 quatre

5 cinc

6 sis

7 set

8 vuit

9 nou

10 deu

11 onze

12 dotze

13 tretze

14 catorze

15 quinze

16 setze

17 disset

18 divuit

19 dinou

20 vint

21 vint-i-un

30 trenta

40 quaranta

50 cinquanta

60 seixanta

70 setanta

80 vuitanta

90 novanta

100 cent

101 cent un

200 dos-cents (dues-centes)

500 cinc-cents

1000 mil

Menu reader

Basic words

Esmorzar To have breakfast

Dinar To have lunch

Sopar To have dinner

Ganivet Knife

Forquilla Fork

Cullera Spoon

CATALAN

Taula Table
Ampolla Bottle
Got Glass
Carta Menu
Sopa Soup
Amanida Salad
Entremesos Hors d'oeuvres
Truita Omelette
Entrepà Sandwich
Torrades Toast
Tapes Tapas
Mantega Butter
Ous Eggs
Pa Bread
Olives Olives
Oli Oil
Vinagre Vinegar
Sal Salt
Pebre Pepper
Sucre Sugar
El compte The bill
Sóc vegetarià/ I'm a vegetarian

Catalan specialities

Amanida catalana Salad served with sliced meats (sometimes cheese)
Arròs a banda Rice with seafood, the rice served separately
Arròs a la marinera Paella: rice with seafood and saffron
Arròs negre "Black rice", cooked in squid ink
Bacallà a la llauna Salt cod baked with garlic, tomato and paprika
Botifarra (amb mongetes) Grilled Catalan pork sausage (with stewed haricot beans)
Calçots Large char-grilled spring onions
Canelons Cannelloni, baked pasta with ground meat and béchamel sauce
Conill all i oli Rabbit with garlic mayonnaise
Crema catalana Crème caramel, with caramelized sugar topping
Escalivada Grilled aubergine/eggplant, pepper/capsicum and onion
Espinacs a la Catalana Spinach cooked with raisins and pine nuts
Esqueixada Salad of salt cod with peppers/capsicums, tomatoes, onions and olives
Estofat de vedella Veal stew

Faves a la Catalana Stewed broad beans, with bacon and botifarra
Fideuà Short, thin noodles (the width of vermicelli) served with seafood
Fuet Catalan salami
Llenties guisades Stewed lentils
Mel i mató Curd cheese and honey
Pa amb tomàquet Bread (often grilled), rubbed with tomato, garlic and olive oil
Pollastre al cava Chicken with cava sauce
Pollastre amb gambes Chicken with prawns
Postres de músic Cake of dried fruit and nuts
Salsa romesco Spicy sauce (with chillis, nuts, tomato and wine), often served with grilled fish
Samfaina Ratatouille-like stew (onions, peppers/capsicum, aubergine/eggplant, tomato), served with salt cod or chicken
Sarsuela Fish and shellfish stew
Sípia amb mandonguilles Cuttlefish with meatballs
Suquet de peix Fish and potato casserole
Xató Mixed salad of olives, salt cod, preserved tuna, anchovies and onions

Cooking terms

Assortit Assorted
Al forn Baked
A la brasa Char-grilled
Fresc Fresh
Fregit Fried
A la romana Fried in batter
All i oli Garlic mayonnaise
A la plantxa Grilled
En escabetx Pickled
Rostit Roast
Salsa Sauce
Saltat Sautéed
Remenat Scrambled
Del temps Seasonal
Fumat Smoked
A l'ast Spit-roasted
Al vapor Steamed
Guisat Stewed
Farcit Stuffed

Desserts/Postres

Pastís Cake
Formatge Cheese

Flam Crème caramel
Gelat Ice cream
Arròs amb llet Rice pudding
Tarta Tart
Yogur Yoghurt

Drinks

Cervesa Beer
Vi Wine
Xampan/cava Champagne
Cafè amb llet Large white coffee
Cafè tallat Small white coffee
Descafeinat Decaf
Te Tea
Xocolata Drinking chocolate
Granissat Crushed ice drink
Llet Milk
Orxata Tiger nut drink
Aigua Water
Aigua mineral Mineral water
Zumo Juice

Fish and seafood/ Peix i marisc

Anxoves/Seitons Anchovies
Calamarsets Baby squid
Orada Bream
Cloïses Clams
Cranc Crab
Sipia Cuttlefish
Lluç Hake
Llagosta Lobster
Rap Monkfish
Musclos Mussels
Pop Octopus
Gambes Prawns
Navalles Razor clams
Salmó Salmon
Bacallà Salt cod
Sardines Sardines
Llobarro Sea bass
Llenguado Sole
Calamars Squid
Peix espasa Swordfish
Tonyina Tuna

Fruit/Fruita

Poma Apple
Plàtan Banana
Raïm Grapes
Meló Melon
Taronja Orange
Pera Pear
Maduixes Strawberries

Meat and poultry/Carn i aviram

Bou Beef
Embotits Charcuterie
Pollastre Chicken
Xoriço Chorizo sausage
Pernil serrà Cured ham
Llonganissa Cured pork sausage
Costelles Cutlets/chops
Ànec Duck
Pernil dolç Ham
Xai/Be Lamb
Fetge Liver
Llom Loin of pork
Mandonguilles Meatballs
Porc Pork
Conill Rabbit
Salsitxes Sausages
Cargols Snails
Bistec Steak
Llengua Tongue
Vedella Veal

Vegetables/Verdures i llegums

Carxofes Artichokes
Albergínia Aubergine/eggplant
Faves Broad/lima beans
Carbassó Courgette/zucchini
All Garlic
Mongetes Haricot beans
Llenties Lentils
Xampinyons Mushrooms
Cebes Onions
Patates Potatoes
Espinacs Spinach
Tomàquets Tomatoes
Bolets Wild mushrooms

SMALL PRINT

Publishing Information
Sixth edition 2024

Distribution
UK, Ireland and Europe
Apa Publications (UK) Ltd; sales@roughguides.com
United States and Canada
Ingram Publisher Services; ips@ingramcontent.com
Australia and New Zealand
Booktopia; retailer@booktopia.com.au
Worldwide
Apa Publications (UK) Ltd; sales@roughguides.com

Special Sales, Content Licensing and CoPublishing
Rough Guides can be purchased in bulk quantities at discounted prices. We can create special editions, personalised jackets and corporate imprints tailored to your needs. sales@roughguides.com.
roughguides.com

Printed in Czech Republic

This book was produced using **Typefi** automated publishing software.

A catalogue record for this book is available from the British Library

The publishers and authors have done their best to ensure the accuracy and currency of all the information in **Pocket Rough Guide Barcelona**, however, they can accept no responsibility for any loss, injury, or inconvenience sustained by any traveller as a result of information or advice contained in the guide.

Rough Guide Credits
Editor: Rachel Lawrence
Cartography: Carte
Picture Editor: Piotr Kala
Picture Manager: Tom Smyth
Layout: Pradeep Thapliyal

Head of DTP and Pre-Press:
Rebeka Davies
Original design: Richard Czapnik
Head of Publishing: Sarah Clark

Acknowledgements
Enormous thanks, as ever, to the indefatigable Mary Ann Gallagher for her research assistance, and to Rachel Lawrence for endless patience. Thanks, too, to Tess O'Donovan for tolerating my absences with good grace.

Help us update

We've gone to a lot of effort to ensure that this edition of the **Pocket Rough Guide Barcelona** is accurate and up-to-date. However, things change – places get "discovered", opening hours are notoriously fickle, restaurants and rooms raise prices or lower standards. If you feel we've got it wrong or left something out, we'd like to know, and if you can remember the address, the price, the hours, the phone number, so much the better.

Please send your comments with the subject line "**Pocket Rough Guide Barcelona Update**" to mail@uk.roughguides.com. We'll credit all contributions and send a copy of the next edition (or any other Rough Guide if you prefer) for the very best emails.

Photo Credits

(Key: T-top; C-centre; B-bottom; L-left; R-right)

A Tu Bola 61
Adrià Goula Sarda 117
Bosc de les Fades 31
Chris Christoforou/Rough Guides 18T, 21T, 25, 49, 52, 56, 62, 63, 66, 67, 72, 83, 87, 108, 112, 119, 129, 135, 139, 148/149
Christian Schriefer/Picnic 79
Dreamstime 109, 114, 158/159
Greg Gladman/Apa Publications 126
iStock 2TL, 2BR, 4, 10, 11B, 20B, 24, 33, 38, 64, 80, 86, 99, 104, 105, 120, 133, 138, 141, 142, 143, 147
Joan Valera/Compartir 13C
kcakduman/Flickr 12/13B

Ramon Casas i Carbó/Museu del Modernisme Català 113
Roger Mapp/Rough Guides 14B, 15T, 20T, 27, 30, 32, 40, 41, 45, 47, 51, 53, 57, 73, 78, 90, 95, 100, 124, 125, 132
Shutterstock 1, 2BL, 2C, 5, 6, 11T, 12T, 12B, 14T, 15B, 16B, 16T, 17B, 17T, 18C, 18B, 19T, 19C, 19B, 20C, 21C, 21B, 22/23, 28, 29, 36, 39, 42, 43, 44, 46, 50, 58, 59, 60, 68, 69, 71, 74, 75, 76, 82, 85, 88, 89, 92, 93, 94, 97, 98, 101, 102, 103, 110, 111, 116, 123, 127, 128, 144, 145, 146
Taverna del Clinic 118
Tim Kavenagh/Rough Guides 136

Cover Park Guell **Sergii Figurnyi/Shutterstock**

Index

NOTES

NOTES